Pillsbury's Family Weight Control Cook Book

Menus and recipes
low in calories,
high in nutrition.

pillsbury publications

Dear Homemaker:

From the newest addition to our family of Pillsbury Consumer Service Kitchens, our Publications Center is proud to give you information and recipes on one of the most timely subjects in the United States.

This new kitchen and staff are responsible for all of the carefully tested recipes contained in this book. They have been prepared with equipment and ingredients just as you would prepare them in your home. This is our way to be sure your results will be excellent.

The training and experience of the Publications Center staff qualify them to give you a broad range of help in maintaining proper eating for good health. We have also sought the advice of experts in the field of nutrition.

Included is dieting information which covers the broad spectrum of concerns homemakers continually talk to us about. We have given you information on nutrition which we feel will make this subject come alive in your food purchasing and preparation. Menus with calorie counts are one of the most sought after food subjects. We've given you a great variety of these.

We feel this book contains all the information and recipe material to maintain good eating and good health for you and your family.

Cordially,

Barbara Thornton

Barbara Thornton, Director
Consumer Service Kitchens

Contents

4

Eat Wisely & Well

Losing weight doesn't have to be a hunger strike!

You can slim down to your desirable weight and keep it — simply by choosing foods wisely. By selecting a balanced menu, you can look ahead to a trim figure and enjoy eating at the same time. Whether you're already slim and want to stay that way or have extra pounds you'd like to lose, **a wise plan of food selection can be the key to many happy, slender years.**

If you're overweight, chances are it's obvious. Telltale bulges that make zippers hard to zip and buttons hard to button are visible to others even though you can only see them in a mirror. Perhaps your favorite suit that you bought last year hangs in the closet now because there isn't enough of it to cover you. Maybe your husband casually mentions how attractive he thought you were **when** you had your girlish figure. Small excesses of calories that come from an extra helping here and there, from the extra snacks while watching television, or just from the way food is prepared, add up slowly, but surely nevertheless, to add on inches.

Weight usually isn't gained overnight, and likewise, isn't lost overnight, either. The eating habits you establish within your family can be ones that provide the nutrients needed for healthy living and still keep calories within a reasonable range. Or, they can be ones that trap you and your family in the never ending battle against weight control.

Since you are, most likely, the one who purchases and prepares the food your family eats, **it is up to you to guide your family in developing sensible eating habits.** Teach your family the eating habits that will provide them with the nutrients and energy they need for healthful living.

Balance is the key — sensibly consuming a variety of foods in reasonable quantities can keep you and your family shapely and filled with vitality and a great sense of well-being. It can also add happy, healthy years to your lives. **What better gift could you give your family?**

The Image of You

We are all aware that, unfortunately, some foods are loaded with something called calories, and that those foods tend to load hips and waistlines with something called fat. However, calories aren't just heaped in staggering quantities in foods-you-like-but-shouldn't-eat; they're in all foods. **Calories are a measurement of the potential energy which a food can give you when you eat it and the rate at which you burn it up.** All foods contain some calories, and all activity burns up some calories. The food you eat is converted to energy (calories) by digestion and is used by the body as it is needed for activity and other forms of operation. If energy or calories are present in a larger quantity than the body needs at that time, the remainder is converted to fat and stored until a time when it is needed. This is when weight is gained. Occasionally, the body will need more energy for activity than the food which was eaten that day contains. When this happens, the stored fat is converted to energy and is made available to the body for use. This is when weight is lost. The trick is to balance what you eat with enough activity to keep the calories you take in and the calories your body expends approximately equal. **To loose weight, activity (the amount of calories burned up) must be more than the number of calories eaten.** Our easy modern life in which we ride rather than walk, depend on automatic equipment, and sit at desks and files all day makes us prone to be overweight. We simply require fewer calories than we eat.

To lose weight, you must eat fewer calories than your body burns. The rate at which you lose weight will depend on the number of calories you subtract from your diet each day. A reduction of about 3,500 calories is necessary to produce the loss of one pound of body weight. To lose 2 lbs. a week, you will have to eat 7,000 calories less than your body expends. That's 1,000 calories less per day. If your normal caloric need were 2,200 calories a day, you would need to reduce your calories to 1,200. This number of calories is sufficient to

provide you with the vitamins and minerals that are essential to health and yet is low enough to produce weight loss.

You can get a general idea of the **number of calories you use in daily activity** by this easy method. Multiply your weight by 16 for a woman or by 18 for a man. The answer will be approximately the number of calories you burn daily. If you are fairly inactive (especially older adults), you will probably need fewer calories than this method shows. However, if you are very active, you will tend to burn more calories.

Unless you are aware that your activity is noticeably higher or lower than normal, assume that it is average. For example, the desirable weight for a woman who is 5 feet 4 inches and has an average build, page 8, is 122 lbs. She will use about 122 x 16 (or about 1,950) calories each day.

The desirable weight for a man who is 5 feet 10 inches tall (with an average build) is 159 lbs. If his activity is about average, he will use 159 x 18 (or about 2,860) calories per day.

Men usually have a higher caloric need than women because they are larger and because a greater part of their bodies is lean (muscle) tissue rather than fat. More energy is used when there is a greater proportion of lean tissue because more calories are transformed in the muscle tissue to energy for the body to use.

Age also influences the number of calories needed. Growth periods, (especially infancy, adolescence and pregnancy) are periods during which the caloric requirement is high. Naturally as an adult grows older, the body needs fewer calories to function.

Keep a record for a day or two of everything you eat and the calories you consume. How does it compare with the number of calories which your body uses?

After you have reached your desirable weight, you can use this method to figure the number of calories you need to eat to maintain your slimness.

Body types and genetic factors that are inherited through birth will determine a person's affinity for weight gain. A person with large bones is likely to have more muscle and consequently tend to weigh more than a person with small bones. This is an easy out for the dieters who would like to loose weight but just don't want to go to the trouble to reduce calories. Tell yourself that you were destined to be heavy because of your large frame, and there's no need for you to go on a diet.

But take a look in your mirror — a realistic look. Your mirror doesn't lie. If you have bulges of fat, you're carrying around extra weight — whether you're large, medium or small framed. Excess fat that collects to make "spare tires" and "love handles" is pretty hard to rationalize as part of your desirable body weight.

Weight is likely to accumulate in various places on individuals. Because women have normal fatty deposits in breasts, hips and thighs, it's easy to store a little more in those areas than is necessary. Tummies and waistlines tend to expand in both men and women especially as activity and metabolism rates decline as a person gets older. Under the chin and on the back of the neck are also areas where both men and women tend to store excess fatty tissue. It's apparent that two or more individuals of the same height and weight can be well-nourished, underweight and overweight depending on the individual body structure of each. Your desirable weight, however, is usually that which you weighed or weigh between the ages of 25 and 30, provided you were in good health and neither over or underweight in terms of your particular body build. A man at 25 and a woman at 20 have most likely reached maximum physical growth — any gain after that is usually "excess fat".

Find out what your body build is. **Wrists and ankles can give you a good indication of your bone size because these are areas where little fat or muscle hides the bone.**

Check the following chart according to your height and body build; compare your present weight with the desirable weight. Now you take it from here. The decision is yours to make if you're overweight. You have about three choices. You can stay at the weight you are now, maybe gaining a little from time to time. You can take some off for awhile, and maybe put it back on later when you're tired of your diet. Or, you can make up your mind that you intend to take off the extra weight and keep it off permanently by changing your eating habits so that excess calories aren't plaguing your body and building up excess fat.

No matter which choice you make, this book will become a good friend of yours because it has recipes for food that will satisfy the appetites of non-dieters as well as dieters. But if you choose the last alternative, we're especially glad to have you join the ranks of people who enjoy good food and healthful eating while they're watching their calories and staying slim.

Your body has stored excess calories in the form of fat tissue. To get rid of that tissue, you must either increase your energy output (activity) beyond that which you feed your body, or you must decrease your caloric intake below your activity level. Either way **your body has to draw on the fat reserves for energy and burn it up.** Increasing the amount of activity you do — in general motion or in specific exercises — is especially important in the early stages of a reducing diet. It helps those first few pounds drop off and provides more motivation on the part of the dieter to stick with it. But **exercise alone is not enough to do the whole trick. Eating fewer calories plays the critical role.**

Exercise — regular exercise, that is — gives your body and muscles the good tone that makes you feel ready to tackle anything the day has to offer. An occasional fling does little more than make you stiff and a bit dubious about "punishing" yourself further. Start gradually and work up to more if you're interested in getting your body into top shape (tone and form)! Remember, too, that **weight gain is easier to prevent than to correct;** a little awareness on the part of those who are slender can help insure that they STAY slender!!

We've listed a few types of activity that you're probably familiar with and given the approximate number of calories that they burn up for every fifteen minutes that you do them. You'd have to really keep moving if you intended to lose weight solely on the basis of increased activity. But you can see from the examples given here that **some extra exercise can contribute to the efforts you're putting into reducing calories.**

The range in calories burned allows for differences in persons. Smaller persons will burn less; larger will burn more. Some people participate more energetically than others; they, too, will use more calories. In general, calorie expenditures for men will tend to be toward the upper limits, and those for women toward the lower. **More strenuous activities will burn more calories than those not requiring as much physical exertion.**

DESIRABLE WEIGHTS FOR WOMEN
(Without clothing)

Height (Without shoes)	Small	Average	Large
5'	100	109	118
5' 1"	104	112	121
5' 2"	107	115	125
5' 3"	110	118	128
5' 4"	113	122	132
5' 5"	116	125	135
5' 6"	120	129	139
5' 7"	123	132	142
5' 8"	126	136	146
5' 9"	130	140	150
5' 10"	133	144	156
5' 11"	137	148	161
6'	141	152	166

DESIRABLE WEIGHTS FOR MEN
(Without clothing)

Height (Without shoes)	Small	Average	Large
5' 3"	118	129	141
5' 4"	122	133	145
5' 5"	126	137	149
5' 6"	130	142	155
5' 7"	134	147	161
5' 8"	139	151	166
5' 9"	143	155	170
5' 10"	147	159	174
5' 11"	150	163	178
6'	154	167	183
6' 1"	158	171	188
6' 2"	162	175	192
6' 3"	165	178	195

"Food and Your Weight." Home and Garden Bulletin No. 74. U.S.D.A., August 1969.

Calories per l5 minutes

20 to 25

Reading
Writing
Watching t.v. or movies
Sewing
Eating
Typing
Playing cards
Office work done sitting
Activities done while sitting
    that require little or no arm movement

27 to 40

Preparing and cooking food
Doing dishes
Hand laundering
Ironing
Dusting
Walking slowly
Office work done standing
Rapid typing
Personal care
Activities done while sitting that are
    more strenuous

43 to 60

Making beds
Sweeping
Mopping & scrubbing
Light gardening or carpentry
Walking moderately fast
Activities done while sitting that
    require more vigorous arm movement

65 to 85

Heavy work
Heavy scrubbing and waxing
Hanging out clothes
Walking fast
Bowling
Golfing
Gardening
Table tennis
Skating
Bicycling at moderate speed

85 and more

Swimming
Tennis
Running
Bicycling fast
Dancing
Skiing
Football

"Food and Your Weight." Home and Garden Bulletin No. 74. U.S.D.A.,
August 1969.

Many different types of diets are constantly bombarding us in magazines, newspapers and other media. Many of these promise that you can eat as much as you want and still lose weight or that you'll "lose-weight-fast". Some of them give you the idea that calories in food can be ignored. **You can ignore calories, if you want, but your body counts every one you feed it.**

Fast weight loss is promised by other diets. Many times these diets feature one or two foods at the expense of others. This can leave you with a deficiency in the essential nutrients which are provided by those other foods. **Diets that are especially high in one food** (high-carbohydrate, high-protein, or high-fat) **are most likely low in another type of food.** Pages l8 to 24 explain the various types of nutrients and the reasons your body needs all of them for proper functioning. Eliminate most of the carbohydrates in your diet and you'll probably be on a high-fat diet.

A crash diet may enable you to lose several pounds rapidly. Chances are, though, that you'll rapidly get tired of the lack of variety in your meals — and will go off of the diet out of sheer boredom. Or, maybe you'll be able to exist on mushrooms and celery for several days. But by the third or fourth day, you have no energy, crave every food imaginable, and go on an eating binge. That's a good way to GAIN WEIGHT rather than lose weight!

Other fad diets recommend restricting water from your diet. Several pounds are all that can be lost this way, and rarely does that loss actually include any fat tissue. Most of the cells and fluids in the body contain a high percentage of water. In order to maintain the correct balance of minerals inside and outside the cells, to provide enzymes and hormones a media in which to operate, to ensure proper elimination of body wastes, your body needs water.

Sweating is also occasionally used as a means for reducing. Whether it's from exercise, a hot bath, or sitting in a steam room, this method can only get rid of a pound or two. Water is part of your total body weight, and this type of loss is easily replaced the next time you take a drink. **Body fat itself can't be steamed or evaporated off.**

Health spas also feature "spot reducing". Massage — by vibrators or by hand — may make you feel great, but it has little value for reducing. **Fat deposits won't rub off** by rollers or gadgets that make you shake and shimmer. This kind of passive exercise requires very little energy to be used up by the body, and consequently, uses up few excess calories. Because the muscles aren't used much either, exercise in which the effort is provided by a machine or by another person is not of much value for toning body muscle either. If these "spot-reducing" techniques seem to result in weight loss, it's probably because the individual has eaten less or gotten more exercise in which it was necessary to use body energy.

Drugs for reducing are sometimes prescribed by doctors; these are potent drugs and are only available by prescription. Most of these drugs function by acting on the satisfaction center of the brain to produce a decrease in appetite. This can be helpful in the beginning stages of a diet when the dieter is learning to be satisfied with a smaller amount of food.

A thyroid substance, which speeds up the burning of food energy (calories), is also occasionally prescribed. A deficiency in thyroid substances can make a person sluggish and give him a tendency toward overweight; thyroid hormone supplements can compensate for this deficiency. However, most overweight people have properly functioning thyroid glands (tests by a doctor are necessary to show deficiencies). Thyroid hormones which are in addition to a normal level can be hazardous.

If it's 5 to 10 pounds you're interested in losing, drugs aren't usually necessary. **But if you're interested in losing over 10 pounds or are having problems reducing by yourself, see your doctor.** If he prescribes drugs, take them; but if he doesn't, you may do yourself injustice by experimenting with them.

Miracles that will make you instantly slim may be appealing. But to conquer the weight battle permanently, you'll need to establish a permanent, low calorie, nutritious pattern of eating — for the dieters in your family, as well as the non-dieters.

If you are serious about weight control, it's more than just losing weight for brief periods. **In order to keep the weight off, you must look at weight control as a long-range pattern — making low calorie, sensible eating a habit.**

SPECIAL PROBLEMS IN REDUCING

You have been eating for a good many years already and most likely have established some eating patterns for yourself. To understand what those are, it might help to keep a record for several days of the things which you eat. Or, perhaps you can simply recall the types of food you usually include in your diet. In either case, make an estimate of the number of calories your body takes in and categorize the foods according to the basic four food groups in page 22. From this comparison, **you can evaluate your deficiencies and excesses and begin to make changes or substitutions where they're necessary.** Some of these will be easy to make; others may take some dedication on your or other dieters' parts.

Many people who are away from home during the day find it necessary to eat lunch in restaurants. Many restaurants make it easy for you by featuring low calorie plates on their menus. But even those that don't list a low calorie menu as such usually offer a wide enough choice that you can select a nutritious meal that is not high in calories.

If you are a frequent customer of the restaurant and/or know one or two of the waiters well, they will be more than happy to assist you in selecting your calorie counting meal from their menu. Feel free to **ask how a dish is prepared.** For instance, is the roast beef served with gravy over it? If so, you'd like yours without the gravy, please! Keep in mind the fact that you are purchasing the services of the waiter and the cook, along with your food, when you patronize a restaurant. As a customer, **you have the right to be satisfied and in doing so to place your order as you wish.**

Establishing yourself as a regular customer at several restaurants may make your calorie-conscious ordering easier. Let the waiters know that you are interested in curtailing calories. Especially if they know that you are a regular customer, they will be glad to help in any way they can. After all, that's their job!

There are several guidelines which you can keep in mind when selecting from a menu. You already know the approximate calorie range that you want to stay within, and you have some idea of the foods from the basic food groups wihch you need to include. Select your meal within this framework.

Fried foods and foods with sauces are usually quite high in calories. Unless you know that you can separate the calories (i.e., taking the skin off of fried chicken, etc.), you would be wise to avoid these foods. Main dishes that are roasted, broiled, baked, or steamed are your best bets.

Garnishes such as fried onion rings sometimes appear beside the main dish you've ordered. You may think to yourself that since you've paid for them, you might as well eat them. However, you would do better to leave them on your plate than to add them to your waistline.

Trim off all excess fat from cuts of meat, and stick to meats that are served "au jus" or plain, instead of with gravy.

Some cuts of meat served by restaurants weigh more than 3 or 4 oz. (an average serving). Estimate the size of your serving and count all of the calories from it, or eat only part of it and take the rest home.

Order your vegetables (potatoes especially) plain. If you must have butter, order it separately. This way you will know exactly how many calories you are adding.

Salads — both with the meal and as a main dish — are a great boon to dieters. Beware, though, of the calories that can be added with salad dressings. Ask for the dressing to be brought separately. You can control the amount this way. Lemon juice or plain vinegar can even be used as dressings by themselves and add very few calories.

Many restaurants serve a basket of rolls and lots of butter for you to nibble on while you're waiting for your meal. Some even include trays of hors d'oeuvres. If these are low calorie relishes, you can help yourself. But don't let your voracious eyes talk yourself into having several rolls loaded with butter. If waiting until your meal comes requires more will power than you have developed so far, a low calorie appetizer, such as tomato juice, clear soups, melon, etc., can keep you occupied until the rest comes.

If you have extra calories to spare in your selection of lunch and want to use them for dessert, fruit dishes that don't have sugar added, plain gelatin desserts, angelfood or sponge cakes, or small amounts of ice milk or sherbet are good choices. A final cup of coffee or tea can even be a dessert for you if you savor each sip before going back to work.

Eating out in the evening can be handled in much the same way as lunch. **Evening dining usually places more emphasis on the social aspects of eating.** Enjoying the company of those you are with is probably the very reason you are there. If you are starting your evening with a cocktail, don't forget that alcohol calories count, too. **The calories in alcohol are actually "empty calories"** — they don't contain the vitamins or other nutrients which your body needs for proper functioning; all they have to offer is calories. While the calories in alcohol can't be stored in the body as fat tissue, this doesn't mean that they go unnoticed. The body quickly uses the calories in alcohol for energy; and while it is doing this, the calories in other foods you're eating — in protein, carbohydrates, and fats — are not being used. This means that these other calories, if they are in excess of what your body needs for energy, will be stored as fat tissue.

The calories in alcoholic beverages can be easily figured. Labels on the bottles tell you the "proof" of liquor. Each ounce contains as many calories as its proof. For example, one ounce of 86-proof whiskey contains 86 calories.

Mixers, such as fruit juices or carbonated beverages, also contain calories that you need to include. Water, ice cubes, and carbonated water are free of calories; dry wine, beer and champagne are among the lower caloried alcoholic beverages. Some of the calories for cocktails are included on page 139.

In this sample menu, good choices for the dieter are in blue. Dishes like these are probably available from the restaurants you know. **Exercise a little courtesy in the way you approach the waiters or waitresses, and they will be more than happy to give you any help they can.**

Choose selectively from the menu and order with tact and diplomacy. **Feel free to order your food exactly as you want it.** Don't be shy in talking candidly with the waiter because you feel embarrassed to make it known that you are watching calories. The bulges you are trying to get rid of show all over your body. Ignoring them won't make them disappear. If you need an alibi, though, tell the waiter you must have your food this way because of an allergy or such. In any case, stand your ground. **It's your fat you're trying to get rid of, and only you can do it!**

STONE HEARTH / MENU

Complete Meals

BLACK POT SPECIAL . . . Rich Soup Made with Beef, Carrots, Onions, Potatoes, Cabbage, Turnips, Barley, Herbs and Spices, Tossed Salad, Rye Bread

CHEF'S SPECIAL . . . Baked Ham with Raisin Sauce, Sweet Potatoes, Buttered Brussels Sprouts, Lettuce Wedge, Roll

BAKED SWORDFISH STEAK . . . Lemon Butter, Parsley Potato, Brussels Sprouts, Jello Salad, Roll

BRAISED SHORT RIBS WITH CARROTS AND ONIONS . . . Whipped Potatoes, Buttered Brussels Sprouts, Tossed Salad, Roll

COLD ROAST BEEF . . . Chilled Potato Salad, Tomato Slices, Coleslaw, Crisp Relishes, Roll

ROASTED HALF CHICKEN . . . Cranberry Sauce, Potato Salad, Sliced Eggs and Tomatoes, Pickle, Roll

GOLDEN FRIED GULF SHRIMP . . . Breaded Fried Shrimp on Toast with French Fried Potatoes, Cocktail or Tartar Sauce, Tossed Salad, Roll

ROAST SLICED SIRLOIN OF BEEF . . . Red Wine Sauce, Whipped Potatoes, Vegetable Du Jour, Tossed Salad, Roll

CHOPPED SIRLOIN STEAK . . . Chopped Sirloin Steak Broiled to Order, French Fried Potatoes, Sliced Tomatoes, Tossed Salad

Entrée Salads

CHEF'S SALAD . . . Crisp Garden Greens with Strip of Turkey, Ham, Swiss Cheese, Egg and Tomato Quarters

BOUILLABAISSE SALAD BOWL . . . Fresh Garden Greens Topped with Seafood Tidbits and Chef's Special Garnishes

WEIGHT WATCHER . . . Molds of Cottage Cheese on Lettuce Surrounded by Fresh Fruit and Berries

Sandwiches

FRENCH DIP . . . Hot Roast Beef Slices on Pumpernickel, Au Jus, Coleslaw

MONTE CRISTO . . . Three Decker with Ham, Chicken, and Swiss Cheese, Served Hot with Sour Cream and Strawberry Dressing

ENGLISH MUFFINS . . . Toasted English Muffins with Grilled Canadian Bacon and Tangy Cheddar Cheese Sauce, Coleslaw

HOT OPEN-FACED TURKEY SANDWICH . . . Sliced Hot Turkey Breast on Whole Wheat, Supreme Sauce, Spiced Fruit

Beverages

Buttermilk
Milk
Skim Milk
Coffee
Tea

Desserts

Assorted French Pastries
Grapes Romanoff
Cheese with Crackers
Fruit Pies
Pineapple Cream Pie
Lemon or Raspberry Sherbet
Ice Cream
Cheese Cake
Angelfood Cake
Fruit Cup

Entertaining friends in your home or going to theirs for dinner can also present problems to the weight watcher. Some hostesses feel that having guests warrants special dishes or extra preparation. One of the main reasons that friends like to get together is to enjoy each other's company. Food is actually a secondary character in this play. **For the first several weeks while you're getting accustomed to your new, sensible pattern of eating, it might be easier for you to refuse invitations to eat out until you become more sure of yourself and your will power.** Once you've passed this stage, though, you can look forward to enjoying these occasions with your friends.

When you accept an invitation, you can make it easier on yourself as well as your hostess if you tell her that you're not heavy eaters and that she really doesn't need to go to a lot of trouble for you. Your hostess will appreciate knowing that she doesn't have to knock herself out in getting ready, and will understand when you take modest servings. Keep the upper hand on your cocktails or hors d'oeuvres by leaving a small amount in your glass or a few morsels on your napkin. These will leave you free to say you're not ready for more yet — **a clever way to be a gracious guest and still stay within your calorie limits.** When you serve yourself, go easy on dishes with sauces or lots of butter; help yourself to low calorie vegetables or relishes. If your hostess is the type that encourages you to take additional servings, you can avoid an awkward situation by eating slowly so that you're just finishing your first serving when others are finishing their seconds. Or, explain to your hostess that you're not accustomed to such elaborate meals, that hers was delicious, and you've enjoyed every bit of it.

If you let your host and hostess know that you're enjoying their hospitality, they won't even notice that you're dieting.

When it's your turn to entertain, do it with confidence. If you're having close friends over, you can even let them know that you are going to fix some of your new low calorie recipes for them. Since so many people are watching their weight now, **you're doing your guests a favor in serving a nutrition-packed, low calorie meal.**

We've given several examples of menus you might serve for guests on pages 38 to 53. These are just suggestions, and you will undoubtedly have your own combinations of favorites which you will want to serve. From the ideas we've given, you can get the gist of planning the basic menu with the dieters in mind, then adding other foods for those who tend to be heavy eaters. Start by planning a menu that includes a main dish, a vegetable and a salad (or two vegetables, if you prefer). Add a clear soup, a low calorie beverage, or a fruit dish for an appetizer. Or, begin your meal with a salad course. Include a starchy vegetable or hot rolls for the heavy eaters. And complete the occasion with an elegant, low calorie dessert. Both you and your guests will finish dinner with satisfied stomachs — without that groggy stuffed-to-the-gills feeling.

Meals that include dishes which can be made ahead or which require little last-minute preparation allow you to spend more time with your guests before dinner. Set your table with an interesting centerpiece, page 29 — one that you've made or that has an interesting story behind it. **An attractive setting and friendly atmosphere go a long way in making any meal elegant as well as enjoyable.** Plan your preparation schedule carefully so that all of your dishes are ready to serve at the same time; do as much as possible ahead of time, and both you and your meal will come off graciously.

Entertaining is the perfect situation to include lovely garnishes, page 30, with your dishes. They add a quick and special touch that makes the meal look like it came straight from one of the all-time greatest chefs.

Maybe you've gone on diets before but have given up after a short time because you just didn't want to fix separate meals for yourself and for your family. **By using the sensible eating plan, the dieters and the non-dieters can eat essentially the same meal, with only a few changes.**

The first few pounds will probably come off easily. That's to be expected. Other fat that's been there longer will require more time. In the meantime, **you will probably experience weight plateaus — periods during which you are still eating low calorie foods but not losing additional body weight.** These periods are normal, so don't lose your morale over them. Another drop in weight is just around the corner when you hit a weight plateau.

While you're on a reducing diet, your body is working hard to burn off energy stored as fat; it works harder doing this than it does in converting food to energy. During a weight plateau, you temporarily stop losing weight because your body has to rest. During this time, your body redistributes fat. **It's a sign that your body is adapting to the lower calorie intake,** and the readjustment is necessary to maintain the previous loss in weight.

The number of pounds you lose per week may also vary periodically — even though your calorie intake remains the same. This is normal and is often due to variations in water retention. **You may still be losing fat while your weight stays the same.**

Every pint of water retained in the body is equal to one pound of weight. (This is different from fat and can actually hide fat that is lost during this period.) The quantity of salt eaten, liquids consumed, and fluid retention connected with the menstrual cycle all play a part in this. Variations due to fluids retained are greatest during the first stages of weight loss. Don't let them discourage you! **If you continue to watch your calories, the fat will continue to be used up — regardless of the fluids your body temporarily holds.**

As you begin your reducing diet, there may be times when your will power fails you. **Morale boosters are very important during those times.** Don't let one weakening of your will power lead you to rationalizing that you really didn't want to be on a diet anyway. When you taught your children to walk, you encouraged them to get back up after they had fallen and to try again. The self confidence that you build in yourself in getting back on your diet after you've gone off of it can make your will power that much stronger the next time.

If tricks like pasting a picture of yourself "before" on the refrigerator door or moving the scales into the kitchen seem to help, use them by all means. **Things that will remind you of your goal** — a new dress in a smaller size, an outline of your goal figure drawn on the mirror, saving a dollar for every pound you lose for a figure-terrific outfit — **can be great encouragement to you.** Gimmicks for losing weight can be found anywhere. However, looking at weight control as a long-term understanding of your calorie needs and the balancing of those needs, you can realize that a starvation followed by a gorging is not the answer. The key to a permanently slim figure lies in establishing sensible eating patterns that allow you to stay within your calorie (energy) needs.

After you've slimmed down to your new figure, you will want to keep it that way permanently. Start by thinking of yourself as a slim person. If your image of yourself is that of an overweight person who has lost a few pounds, it may be easier for you to put those pounds back on again. So, **eat and think like a slim, trim person and you can make it easier to keep those pounds off.**

Figure the number of calories you need according to the method on page 7. Experiment with the new number of calories by adding new foods gradually to your diet. Take a long-term view of your weight and avoid adding a few pounds here and there. **The easiest way to stay trim is to prevent a small weight gain from turning into a larger gain; take off any pounds that reappear right away.**

The eating patterns you've established for yourself and for your family can carry over from your reducing diet to a sensible pattern of eating that will enable you to maintain your weight loss. You alone control the food that enters your mouth, and you alone can make the changes necessary in your eating habits to help you lose weight. When you've reached your goal and see how attractive you really can be, you'll want to keep that full-of-vitality feeling. **Make it a life-time goal to be healthy and slim!**

ENCOURAGEMENTS

When you begin your new reduced calorie pattern of eating, you may notice various responses which your body will make to the change. When you first start a low calorie pattern of eating, it may happen that the change of diet will give you the impression of hunger — not because the quantity of food is too small but because your stomach hasn't yet adapted to the new kind of eating.

A center in the brain controls the feelings of hunger or satisfaction; it works very much like the thermostat which controls heat for your home. Your "appestat" becomes used to a certain quanitity of food. When you've eaten less than this quantity, it makes you feel hungry; when you've had enough to satisfy yourself, you feel full.

If you turn your thermostat up to 90°, your furnace will put out enough heat to bring the temperature up to 90° — even though it may be uncomfortably warm. Many times, we get used to eating more than we need, and so our "appestats" learn to make us feel hungry even when we've already eaten enough to supply the necessary body energy.

Part of the plan in establishing sensible eating habits is to re-teach your "appestat" to want the correct amount of food. In the week or two that this will take, you may think you feel hungry. But, you don't need to feel sorry for your body; it has many calories stored as fat that can be called upon if it needs energy.

It's important not to let your morale get low, though. So if your "appestat" seems hard to re-train, appease it sparingly with something nutritious like skim milk or raw vegetables. Or, save part of your lunch until mid-afternoon if that helps. Stay with it — once you have programmed your appetite, the majority of the struggle is over!

Another pitfall in dieting comes from boredom with low calorie food. If you eat the same foods day after day, you're bound to crave other foods. And that craving can be just the thing to send you on an eating binge that will devastate several weeks of calorie counting. Avoid this and build lots of variety into your meals. Try new and different ways of preparing food; try new foods. We've included lots of new recipes for you and have also given you some guidelines for using other recipes and choosing ones that will be low in calories. Don't allow yourself to become weary of your meals. Put a bright change in them with a colorful table setting or centerpiece. Eat someplace unusual — in the living room, in the den, on the patio. Experiment with recipe ideas of your own.

Boredom or anxiety can be an important reason for overeating. If you tend to reach to the refrigerator when you're nervous or scan the cabinets when you've finished the ironing and have time to kill before picking the kids up from school, the hunger you feel may be psychological rather than physical. **Most people go off their diets during periods when they're bored, tense or feeling sorry for themselves.**

When you think you're hungry or when you think the refrigerator door is calling you strongly, stop and evaluate the source of your hunger first. If it's psychological hunger, eating won't satisfy it. If you're bored, find something low calorie to do; if you're anxious about something, lie down and relax every muscle in your body; if you're feeling sorry for yourself, think of your goal to be a slim person. Occasionally, it may really be physical hunger. In that case, have something small that's nutritious and low in calories to hold you just until the next meal.

Other people—who know or don't know about your weight watching—may from time to time present problems to your diet. An overweight friend may encourage you to splurge; maybe she's jealous that you will soon have the slim figure she wishes she had. If you want to keep her company in her overweight, go ahead and let her talk you into splurging. Otherwise, remember your goal and refuse politely. It may occasionally be necessary to remind your hospitable friend that you find it hard to refuse and that she could show what a good friend she is by not teasing your appetite.

Your hostess may have prepared a bridge luncheon of calorie-laden foods. You can handle the situation very quietly and politely by taking very small portions of the fattening foods and helping yourself to the lower calorie foods. If that's not possible, eat only a small portion of each serving. Don't feel that you'll hurt your hostess' feelings if you don't fill up. You can let her know that she's a superb cook and still eat a small portion. If you hate to pass up a fattening treat, think about it as passing up your chance to be slim. **When you are truly committed to becoming slim, your will power will be no problem in refusing.**

Members that make up a family are individuals and have individual needs which need consideration in meal planning. **Children's rapidly developing bodies require more nutrients in relation to their size than do adults.** Awake or asleep, running or resting, at school or at play, they use their energy with extravagance — not only for physical activity, but for the important business of growing. So, three well-balanced meals a day plus wisely regulated snacks are a vital investment for today's needs, as well as for future good health.

Wholesome snacks, chosen from nutritious foods (timed so they don't interfere with mealtime appetites) give a necessary lift. Small stomachs sometimes can't wait until grown-up stomachs are ready for food. Cheese slices, vegetable sticks, fresh fruit, a milk drink or ice cream in moderate quantities can help tide the younger child over until mealtime. The wise use of healthy and nutritious foods at an early age can help to establish good, sensible eating patterns for your children. Keeping such foods on hand also reduces the dieter's temptations to snack on cookies or candy that just happen to be stashed away in the cupboard.

Adolescents are also undergoing spurts of growth that require special attention. Favorite foods are doodled on desk tops, discussed on the phone, take the edge off of athletic defeats, and celebrate victories. The last sound at bedtime tends to be the slam of the refrigerator door. The reason behind this is that **teen-agers are growing faster than at any other time of life except infancy.** The growth is not only physical, but psychological, emotional and social as well. In all aspects of their development, the support of balanced nutrition is important for the physical energy that enables them to enjoy life mentally and emotionally.

The bottomless pit of the teen-age appetite is a challenge to your ingenuity and your food budget. Meeting this need wisely, though, will stand him in good stead — not only for satisfying the immediate goal of feeding a fast-growing body, but also for establishing good eating habits for the years to come.

This is an age, also, when some of the urge for independence is expressed in food selection— for lunch at school, snacks after school or on dates. While the habits which you have already established for them will carry them through their eating away from home, you still exert an influence over the meals at home. By supplying your cupboards with healthy, nutritious between-meal foods, you can discourage them against unwise snacking. Many teen-age girls are interested in staying slim; healthy meals that are high in nutrition and low in calories can be a help to them as well.

Adults' diet patterns should be based on individual needs and on the amount of physical activity of the individual. Men whose work is physically strenuous need substantially greater quantities of all foods than desk-bound workers. Outdoor work requires larger amounts of protein and calories than less active indoor work.

Your meals can take into account all of these varying appetites and still allow the dieter to watch calories. **Plan the basic meal with the dieter in mind** — a main dish, a vegetable, and a salad (or two vegetables, if you prefer). Serve a portion of vegetables to the weight watcher before adding butter or sauces. Salad dressings, gravies, sugar, butter and cream can conveniently be served from separate containers at the table so that the dieters can have theirs plain or specially prepared, and others can proceed as usual. If you know the non-dieters will want more than one serving, fix plenty so they can help themselves to seconds. **Additional calories can be added for those not watching weight with starchy vegetables, whole milk products, breads, dressings, sauces and gravies, sweets and other higher calorie foods .**

By learning how to supplement a reducing diet, you're preparing yourself for an easy transition from dieting to maintenance. After you've achieved your slim figure, you'll want to continue the sensible eating patterns you've established. By expanding the portions slightly or adding a few other foods to the meal, you can make use of the recipes we've included here to **help you stay slim and healthy for a lifetime.**

What you eat is reflected in your general health — the energy you have, your resistance to colds and other minor infections, and your outlook on life. So, good health should be the most important consideration in your choice of food, whether your goal is maintaining the ideal weight you've achieved or to slim down to that goal. **Sensible eating will make you and your family feel great and will give you the energy to enjoy busy days.**

A careless pattern of eating can cause many minor ailments and annoyances. Chipped fingernails, dulled hair, acne, tooth decay, irregularity — these can be influenced by your diet. Perhaps you've felt jumpy, depressed, perhaps shaky and short-winded? Maybe you've been depleting your calcium and iron supply by limiting your breakfast to toast and coffee. You need the same milk and other nutritious foods that your family needs to fortify your body and give you the energy for the day's activities.

Children are constantly exposed to various germs and sicknesses at school. **The nutrients which you build into their meals can give them (or not give them) the resistance they need in order to stay healthy.** A good fortification of vitamins C and A sets up a strong barrier against such annoying illnesses.

Over an extended period of time, an imbalanced eating pattern can lead to serious complications: artherosclerosis from cholesterol, high blood pressure, diabetes. Although we have enough to eat today, malnutrition because of not eating the right kind of foods is still a very serious problem. As a mother, you take inventory of the food which you have on hand, and plan what food you need to buy in order to serve meals to your family. Most all mothers are very busy today — working or participating in many community projects and organizations — making it easy to pay only half-hearted attention to your family's health. But since you DO care about your family and since you are probably the only one whose role it is to oversee their eating, **it's your responsibility to teach them good eating habits and see that they are healthfully fed.**

A Healthy Balance

Not only do you feel better yourself when your body is healthy and full of vigor, but you feel better knowing that your family has all the important nutrients to allow them to enjoy each other. You also have confidence that they have all the vitality they need in order to participate fully in things going on around them. The basic information presented in this book may or may not be new to you, but it's about foods that you are familiar with. When you first began to read, you learned only a few words at a time and have gradually built up the knowledge and fluency which you now have. You may want to approach this information in that way. If much of it is new to you, incorporate it gradually; if you are already familiar with some of it, you can use it more quickly. The same may be true for calories. Look them up for the first week or so; after you've used them several times, you'll begin to remember the approximate range of calories without using the calorie chart.

Balance is the key — sensibly consuming a variety of foods in reasonable quantities can keep you shapely and filled with vitality and a great sense of well-being. It can also add happy, healthy years to your lives. **What better gift could you give your family?**

The cells in your body are chemical in nature. They depend on air, water and food to supply the chemicals they need in order to stay alive and to function properly. The foods which will build vitality into your family are ones that you are probably already acquainted with and have served often. **They contain the essential nutrients — proteins, vitamins and minerals, and the energy yielding fats and carbohydrates.** These are all chemical in nature and usually come from plants and animals. Some of them can be stored in your body to be used later as they are needed; others can't be stored so they must be a part of your daily food intake.

The foods which you eat are changed by digestion (breaking the complex molecules of food down into very simple ones which the cells can use) into these nutrients, which are then carried by your blood to each of the cells. **Each of the nutrients has certain functions in the cells to make your body run efficiently.**

Proteins: Protein must be present in every cell in the body and is used to build new tissue and to maintain and repair old tissue. Growing children have an especially great need for this, but adults need it, too, for hair, nails, teeth, bones, skin, muscle and tissue firmness. Proteins are also needed in the body in order to manufacture enzymes, hormones and antibodies which keep the body processes going and help to fight off infections. Protein can also be burned by the cells for energy. **Meat, eggs, milk and milk products, dried peas and beans, nuts and enriched or whole grain breads and cereals** are important sources of protein. Fruits and vegetables contain some protein also, but not enough to keep the body functioning.

Carbohydrates: Carbohydrates are used in the body primarily as energy. However, they are also important in maintaining intestinal regularity because they give bulk to body wastes so that they can be eliminated properly. Carbohydrates are found abundantly in **dried fruits, potatoes and other starchy vegetables, sugars, and cereal and grains;** but they are also present in **fruits and vegetables.**

Fats: Fats are the most concentrated form of energy. Excess energy from carbohydrates and proteins, as well as fats, that the body can't use is stored as fat. Some of this fat is necessary for insulation of the body against changes from hot to cold; other is used as protective cushioning for vital organs such as the heart and lungs. The rest of it is stored as excess fatty tissue until energy expenditure is high enough or calorie intake is low enough (see page 8) for it to be called into use. Fats are found in **vegetable oils and animal fats. Meat** contains a fairly large amount of fat between the tissues and between muscles. **Milk and milk products and nuts** are also substantial contributors, although skim milk and other low fat dairy products have had most of this fat removed. **Egg yolks, coconut and avocados** are also foods of appreciable fat content.

These three nutrients — proteins, carbohydrates and fats — are the basic ingredients in all foods. Some foods have only one of them; butter, for example, consists only of fats. Other foods, such as vegetables, contain two or even three of these essential nutrients. But in addition to these nutrients, foods also have vitamins and minerals in them. Vitamins become enzymes in digestion and in the use of nutrients by the cells. Minerals are necessary as a part of the chemical structure of the vitamins and of the cells which make up the body.

Vitamin A: Vitamin A is essential to the growth of children and to the general health of adults. It is especially important for healthy skin and vision. Vitamin A is also important inside your body to maintain the linings in your nose, mouth and body cavities. **Liver** tops the list of foods which contain vitamin A; but **sweet potatoes, cantaloupe, dark green leafy vegetables, yellow-orange vegetables, apricots, tomatoes, egg yolk, and milk products** also are good sources.

Vitamin C: Vitamin C cannot be stored by the body, so you need a good supply daily. It is essential for healthy tissue throughout your body, plays an important role in the growth and maintenance of teeth, bones, tissues and blood, and helps in healing wounds. **Citrus fruits, strawberries, tomatoes, cauliflower, cantaloupe, cabbage, broccoli and other green vegetables, potatoes, and green pepper** are all good sources of vitamin C.

B Vitamins: There are several B-vitamins. They are known by their chemical names; thiamine, riboflavin, and niacin are the principle ones.

Thiamine: Thiamine is used in the body to promote growth, good appetite, healthy nerves, and good digestion. It is also essential to make the calories from carbohydrates and fats available for the body to use. Good sources of thiamine are: **lean pork, dried peas and beans, liver, vegetables, enriched and whole grain bread, cereals and grain, poultry and fish** (as well as other meats), **milk and eggs.**

Riboflavin: Riboflavin also plays an important role in making the calories in fats, carbohydrates and proteins available for the body to use; it is necessary for good vision and for growth. Riboflavin is found abundantly in **milk and milk products, liver, lean meat, salmon, eggs, enriched and whole grain bread, cereal and grains, and in green leafy vegetables.**

Niacin: Niacin is important for healthy skin and nerves, and it has been shown to help in preventing nervousness, mental depression, and intestinal disorders. **Dairy products, fish, lean meats, poultry, enriched and whole grain bread, cereals and flour, white potatoes, eggs, peanuts, and almonds** are good sources of niacin.

Vitamin D: Vitamin D is needed by the body to make use of calcium and phosphorus in building strong teeth and bones. It is produced in your skin with the help of the **ultraviolet rays of the sun.** It is also, in some places, added to **milk.**

The minerals which your body needs are a very necessary part of all cells and body fluids. In terms of getting enough to supply your body's needs, calcium, phosphorus, iron and iodine are the most important.

Calcium and Phosphorus: Calcium and phosphorus work together in the body and are important not only to bones and teeth, but also for muscle contraction, nerve functioning. In addition, calcium is important in the clotting of blood. **Milk and milk products, dried peas and beans, leafy green vegetables, salmon, crab and clams** are very good sources of calcium. Phosphorus is found abundantly in dried beans, eggs, milk and other dairy products.

Iron: This mineral is necessary to form hemoglobin — the part of blood which transports oxygen throughout your body. Men and boys usually eat foods that provide enough iron for their bodies. Females, though, require larger amounts of iron because of periodic blood losses in menstruation; too little iron in the blood shows up in a lowered capacity for work and in less vitality for daily activities. **Liver, lean meats, dried beans, dried fruits, eggs, enriched and whole grain bread, flour and cereal, leafy green vegetables and shellfish** contain iron in good quantities; however, supplmentary iron in the form of pills is sometimes necessary.

Iodine: Iodine is required by the thyroid gland to produce a hormone which is essential in regulating the rate at which your body burns up energy. **Seafoods** and foods grown in soil near the seacoast are good sources of iron in the diet; and **iodized salt,** which is widely available, is an excellent source.

The chemical workings of the body are very complex, and science is still baffled by some of the marvels of them. Food, though, is essential to keep the mechanisms in operation. Computing the amount of each vitamin, mineral and nutrients daily to make sure you're feeding your family a balanced diet might be a time-consuming task. **The foods have been grouped, though, in four groups according to the proportions of each of the nutrients which they contain.** By including a specific number of servings every day from each of these groups, you can be quite sure that your body is getting enough nourishment to keep it functioning properly and to keep you feeling good and enjoying life.

Meat, Poultry and Eggs:

Meat, poultry, eggs, fish, nuts, dried beans and peas are included in this category. These foods supply the majority of the protein in the diet, as well as good quantities of iron, minerals and B-vitamins. Infants and adults need foods from this group to maintain health. So, plan to have **two servings a day** from foods of this group. For adolescents and adults, three ounces of cooked, boneless meat, fish or poultry is an average serving. (Children can get the food value they need from one ounce servings.) One egg, 2 tablespoons peanut butter or ½ cup cooked dried beans or peas are about equal in protein to 1 ounce of lean meat.

Milk and Dairy Products:

Foods in this group are good suppliers of vitamins A and D, calcium and riboflavin, and many contain good amounts of protein. Cheese, ice cream, and cottage cheese are some of the forms in which dairy products appear. Foods in this group can also be added to other dishes for variety. Children need at least **three or four glasses of milk a day;** teen-agers, four or more; and adults, two. The following quantities are about equal in calcium content to 8 oz. (1 serving) of **skim milk:** 1¼ cups **cottage cheese,** 1½-inch cube Cheddar **cheese,** and 1 cup **ice cream.**

Breads and Cereals:

Foods in this group provide iron, protein, thiamine, riboflavin, niacin and food energy (calories). The foods included in this group are **enriched, whole grain or restored breads and cereals, baked foods made with enriched or whole grain flour, enriched macaroni, spaghetti, and noodles.** Food value is lost in grains and cereals when the bran and germ are removed in processing. So, these nutrients must be replaced. Some states require food industries to "enrich" and "fortify" these products. If the cereal, bread or flour you buy is labeled **"enriched",** you can assume that the three B-vitamins and iron have been added. Four servings of breads and cereals per day are recommended for good nutrition. Preschoolers' servings will be smaller than adults; adolescents can accommodate more than four servings; and dieters may want to reduce their servings to two.

This is the flexible food group because many of the nutrients provided in this group are available in other groups. This group is especially important for supplying energy foods, though — foods which can be used to give the calories needed for energy. For those not watching calories, the recommended number of servings can be used as a minimum, and additional servings can be added for more food nutrients and energy value (calories).

Other foods not included in these lists can also be a part of your menus. Fats, oils, sugars and their products, as well as non-nutritive beverages (coffee, tea, pop, etc.) can be used to give interest. **The nutritive value in most of these other foods is not high** — although the calories generally are, so they should not be used instead of foods in the food groups. However, they can be added to your meals — in amounts according to the calorie range in which you're working.

Fruits and Vegetables:

Four servings per day of foods in this group are recommended. One serving should be a good source of vitamin C (citrus, tomato, etc.), and one should be a good source of vitamin A (dark green or deep yellow vegetable). Other fruits and vegetables can be used to round out the day's menus; a serving is usually ½ cup. Since some of the vitamins in the foods of this group are dissolved in water or destroyed by heat, use the minimum amount of water to cook these foods and avoid overcooking.

Foods in this group are good sources of vitamin C, vitamin A, and some B-vitamins. Refer to the vitamin explanations, page 21, for the roles they play in body processes. Available fresh, frozen and canned, a wide variety exists in the fruits and vegetables from which you can choose. In addition to vitamins, they contain minerals, roughage for healthy intestinal operation, small amounts of protein and lots of food energy.

Food habits begin when one is very young, and are largely influenced by the habits of the family. Foods that the parents like and that the mother fixes often, as well as family customs, all influence what is eaten regularly and what will become food habits. **Some of the keys to sensible weight reduction and staying slim are to know your health habits; build on the good habits which you already have; and bring in supplements where they are needed.** While you're doing this, you're also building good eating patterns into your children's habits because they develop their attitudes toward food and eating by following your example.

"Variety is the spice of life" — and so it is with food. Favorites are always enjoyed, but they can become problems if they are eaten to the exclusion of other foods. Many a well-intended reducing diet has been abandoned out of sheer boredom with the same foods day after day. **Eating a variety of foods is much more realistic to your everyday eating pattern.** It doesn't do you very much good to go on a starvation diet of milk and celery for two weeks and then return to your former habits of eating heavy desserts and fattening between-meal snacks. **If those foods made you gain weight once, they'll certainly do it again!** If you're in the market for a permanently slim figure, a permanently revised eating pattern is essential. Learning to like a variety of foods is a valuable habit to form. Not only is it easier to serve nutritiously balanced meals, but your wide range of choices gives you room to exert some creativity in your meal planning.

If your family tends to like very few different types of foods, go slowly as you introduce new foods to them. It may take several introductions before they become familiar enough with it to really decide whether or not they like the new flavor. **Here are a few guidelines to make your experimentations more successful:**

- Serve small portions of food. Children, especially, won't be discouraged before they start.

- Serve moderately seasoned food at first. Cultivation of an early taste for lots of salt or sugar may be harmful later on. Children have sensitive taste buds, as it is, and tend to enjoy natural flavors.

- Serve a new food (or one that hasn't been successful before) in a new way or with different foods. Give it a new setting, and it may appear to be a new food.

- When introducing a new food, serve it along with favorite, familiar ones.

- Let your family eat at their own speeds. Children especially haven't yet developed the habit of gulping down their food. Eating slowly can be a great boon to your diet, too. Savoring every bite tends to stretch the portion out and makes it seem as though you're eating more.

The whole family, except infants and those on medically prescribed diets, can usually eat the same basic meals. The **amount** of the various foods which different family members eat should vary according to the size and build of the person, his activity, and his stage of development. Even the dieters can be a part of the meal. **Serve the recommended portions from the basic food groups with the dieter in mind and supplement those servings with others for the non-dieters.**

Calories can be controlled at the same time that food variety and appeal are enjoyed by keeping serving size in mind and by following a few basic guidelines for lower calorie preparation techniques. **By adding as few calories as possible when you prepare foods, you give yourself more leeway in choosing a variety of foods for meals.**

- Eat raw or cooked fruits and vegetables whole or peeled very thinly, whenever possible. The more they are chopped up, the more vitamins are lost during cooking.

- Follow tested recipes to avoid wasteful and distasteful failures.

- Use low or moderate heat for cooking all cuts of meat to reduce shrinkage and preserve juices.

- Learn to use seasonings creatively — but cautiously — for a new twist. Experiment by using small amounts at first, then gradually increasing until desired taste level is achieved.

- Broil, bake, roast or braise meats as often as possible. Fried foods add calories.

- Trim all extra fat from meats before you cook them.

- Use skim milk in cooking instead of milk with higher fat content.

- Use cooking utensils with non-stick finish so that the minimum of fat or oil for cooking is needed.

Planning
Your
Meals

What to have for dinner is a familiar question and a puzzle to many people. Whether you approach meal planning on a weekly or a day-to-day basis, **the main thing to keep in mind is the overall balance of foods.** You know your family's food likes and dislikes and you are familiar with their food habits — what they eat for breakfast, lunch, snacks, or what-have-you. With these in mind, check the basic four food groups to see what vacancies you can fill.

Tastes for food vary widely. In the recipes we've included, you will undoubtedly find some dishes your family will be crazy about and will want included in their menus weekly; others they will prefer on an occasional basis. Learn what turns them on and capitalize on it.

You probably won't want to serve the same dish (even if it **is** their favorite) every night of the week, so keep in mind the other meals you've prepared that week. **Each meal should relate in some way — variety, calories, etc. — to the ones before and the ones after it.** Think of the day's meals as a unit and the week's meals as a series of units; the key to both is the basic four food groups.

Somebody in your family is probably on a diet — most people are these days. If the whole family is dieting, your menu planning is greatly simplified. But most likely, just one or two of you are watching your weight, so you will want to plan meals with the non-dieters in mind, too.

The dishes we've included are not only low in calories, but they're also high in nutrition, so they will serve a double purpose to the weight watcher and can still be enjoyed by the "skinnies", as well.

Keep in mind the quantity of food that the non-dieters in your family like. If you have a thin husband or a growing teenager, either will probably need double servings of everything in order to satisfy him. The serving sizes and the calories for those sizes, which we have placed by every recipe, can serve as a guide to how much the recipe will make. Naturally, calories will be doubled for a double serving. Keep appetites in mind when you decide to prepare the quantity given or to half or double the recipe. Also, keep quantities in mind when you dish up the servings for weight watchers. A cottage cheese and peach salad for lunch can be self-defeating if you eat a whole carton of cottage cheese and consume the entire can of peaches in heavy syrup.

If you're serious about loosing weight or staying slim, you'll want to **anticipate the number of calories for each meal before consuming them.** Gobble up a plate full of macaroni and cheese for lunch before you stop to find out how many calories are in your serving. When you check, you'll probably realize that you've just consumed both your lunch **and** your dinner. With a general — it doesn't need to be rigid — idea of the number of calories you expect to have at each meal, you can pace your eating so that you won't be familiar with hunger pangs. This general gauge will be a great boon to your menu planning, too!

So, what ARE you going to have for dinner? Since you probably put more time into the preparation of dinner meals, let's use that as an example. **Start with the main dish** — whether it be meat, poultry, fish or eggs — and build the rest of the meal around it. Keep in mind the number of calories you want to have for the whole meal when you choose the main dish; a main dish that contains about half of your calories is realistic.

Next, **check our mix 'n match, go-together guide,** page 32, for other dishes to serve with the type of main dish you've chosen. Choose a vegetable and a salad or two vegetables — whichever you prefer—for the calorie counters, and an additional vegetable or starchy food for the non-dieters. The suggestions we've given for go-togethers are just that — suggestions. You may have favorite combinations which your family enjoys; by all means, use those, too. Choose the accompanying dishes with these points in mind:

- **Flavor** — If your main dish is mild in flavor, for example, Broiled Chicken, you will want to include a more strongly flavored vegetable or salad in your menu — Cranberry Mold, maybe. This also gives you a hot-cold temperature variation.

- **Texture** — The celery in Cranberry Mold adds a crunch to your meal, while the chicken provides a chewy texture. For a vegetable, you might want to choose something with a small amount of sauce on it — maybe Mustardy Beans or Mock Carrots in Crème.

- **Appearance** — Think about colors and shapes. As you probably know, the way a particular food looks plays a major role in how much your family will like it. Capitalize on this fact and make your meals treats for the eye as well as the tongue. Garnishes — simple yet colorful — can add snazz and enthusiasm for meals and are clever ways to add variety. Take a look at some of our suggestions, page 30.

If you're still within your calorie allotment for that meal, choose a dessert that coordinates in terms of flavor, texture and appearance, as well as your completion of the basic food requirements. If you feel you need a mid-afternoon snack or a before-bed nibble, save your lunch or dinner dessert to have at that time. Again, **be conscious of your serving sizes.** If you plan to have an extra portion, don't forget to count the extra colories with it. Your body counts every single calorie you feed it — whether you do or not.

Breakfast is probably next in relation to the amount of time you spend in preparation. Consider the same guidelines that you followed in assembling an attractive and appetizing dinner. At an early hour, appearance, flavor and texture variations play an even more vital role in stimulating your family's appetite.

Choose your main dish — whether it be cereal and milk or an egg or meat dish. If the dish is hearty — hot cereal, for example — you may want to serve a refreshing fruit juice with it. On the other hand, if it is less filling, a fruit combination or spiced fruit would lend an exciting contrast.

If you find that a midmorning snack makes the difference between your sanity until lunch and approaching lunch with an appetite that exceeds all human control, skip the fruit or juice at breakfast and have it half way through the morning. If you **keep in mind the total balance which you wish to achieve for the entire day** — calorie and nutritional — you can establish an eating schedule that suits your eating habits best. You have the guidelines to follow in the basic four food groups. Use them to their and your advantage in relation to your particular preferences.

Lunch can be treated much the same way as breakfast. For your husband and others in your family who eat away from home, we've given some helps and hints in pages 36 to 37. **You can help them to know what choices are wise ones by sharing your knowledge of basic food needs with them.** By giving them the rationale behind the inclusion of various types of food, they also can learn to evaluate food in terms of a sensible daily and weekly pattern.

If you pack lunch for them or eat at home yourself, you can play an even larger role in supplying them with the proper foods. Pack nutrition into a lunch box by including fruit, soup, vegetables or milk along with the sandwiches. Airtight storage containers provide an excellent way to pack foods that tend to be juicy. Several types of fruits are even available now in single serving sized cans with snap-top lids. Portable raw vegetables are fun nibblers and are enjoyed by both children and adults. Page 36 contains some low calorie and nutritious lunch box ideas for you. You can adapt these ideas for those not watching calories, too, by supplementing the meal with extra servings or other foods.

For those of you who eat at home and are interested in keeping trim, low calorie leftovers from the night before can be combined — provided you are conscious of the size of servings you're combining — to make a luscious combination plate. Soups (those that aren't creamed,

of course) can be very satisfying if eaten with a fruit or vegetable and milk. If you didn't have toast or cereal for breakfast, you might even want to include crackers or toast with your soup. Main Dish salads, pages 114 to 117, combine many nutritious foods into a tasty and attractive meal. Open-face sandwiches (using a low calorie spread to further reduce calories) can also be included in your lunch menus occasionally. If you know you will crave something to eat when the kids come home from school, save a glass of milk, your fruit, or any other part of your lunch to eat at that time. **Pacing your eating** (if you tend to be a snacker) can make it possible for you to face the next meal without "Vulture's eyes". Snacks aren't necessarily evil if you use them to your advantage instead of to your waistline.

Become acquainted with fruits, vegetables and fruit juices as nutritious snacks and teach their value to your children, as well. Pages 36 to 37 in this chapter contain more ideas for lunches. Use them as ideas, substituting your favorites, and enjoy many interesting lunches.

Combine unusual "go-together" foods. Experiment with new flavor combinations — tomatoes instead of mushrooms in a favorite meat dish or mushrooms instead of tomatoes. Once you get the hang of calories and are able to judge the general range into which various foods come, you can substitute endlessly in menus, as well as in dishes themselves.

Pay special attention to your table, too. Candles, a bowl of autumn gourds, dried or plastic flowers, placemats and colored napkins are only a few of the inexpensive items you can use to dress up your table. Use Susie's latest art project from school as a centerpiece for the table. You can bet you'll have an especially satisfied customer eating at your table that night! We've pictured a few ideas above of type of things you probably have on hand — which will easily adapt into a colorful centerpiece.

Have a good time planning and preparing your meals, and your family will enjoy eating the meals you prepare. Prepare an old favorite in a new way. Convert a stand-by by changing the dishes you serve with it, or transform an ordinary vegetable into a light-hearted salad. Add something extra in the way of garnishes or accompaniments, such as lemon slices or chopped green onion. **The imaginative use of an edible garnish can add new interest to a familiar food and enhance the appetite appeal of any menu.** But edible garnishes don't need to be the extent of your decorating. An unusual serving dish can add both color and texture variety to the appearance of your meal — so can an unusual way of serving the food, such as Fruit Fondue, page 53, where everybody dips his own fruit for dessert.

celery fan

melon balls

fruit-filled fruit cups

radish slices in partially sliced cucumber

vegetable combos with toothpicks secured

turnip painted with food coloring

cucumber wedge dipped in paprika

olives stuffed with colored cream cheese

rutabaga and turnip slices cut with cookie cutters

Keep in mind the total calorie balance you want to achieve for the day when you anticipate the number of calories you or other dieters will have at each meal. (You may do a lot of looking up the first week or so, but eventually you will be able to calculate without looking.) Fit portions of the various food groups into that structure, and enjoy your meals. You'll find ideas for breakfast and lunch dishes, as well as supper and dinner ideas in both the remainder of this chapter and in the recipes. **Bon Apetite!!**

celery sticks in carrot curl

citrus tree

lime slices in lemon

vegetable pieces topped with colored cream cheese

carrot curl rose

carrots cut with cookie cutter

saw-tooth-cut lemon with capers

apple peel rose

radish flowers

lime basket

parsley inserted in partially sliced carrot

kumquat flower

GO TOGETHERS

Beef or Veal

Appetizers: Hot bouillon, fruit cup, melon balls, gingerale and fruit juices

Potato or substitute: Mashed or hearty potatoes, rice pilaf, corn, winter squash

Vegetables: Beets, cauliflower, zucchini, carrots, onions, cabbage, tomatoes, summer squash, artichoke, broccoli, mushrooms

Salads: Tomato aspic, marinated vegetables, tossed green, peach and cottage cheese

Desserts: Fruit gelatin mold, pudding, strawberries or other fruit, fruit combinations

Lamb

Appetizers: Fresh fruit or juice, tomato juice

Potato or substitute: Mashed or parslied potatoes, corn, lima beans, winter squash, peas

Vegetables: Carrots, broccoli, spinach, asparagus, summer squash, artichoke, eggplant

Salads: Apricots, cucumber, pear and other fruits, tossed green

Desserts: Lemon chiffon, sherbet, fruits

Poultry

Appetizers: Sherbet, fruit juice, consommé or broth, relishes

Potato or substitute: Mashed or parslied potatoes, sweet potatoes, peas

Vegetables: Spinach, corn, green beans, Brussels sprouts, peas, celery, turnips, artichoke, broccoli, asparagus, eggplant, beets, okra

Salads: Raw vegetables, Waldorf, cranberry, carrot, lettuce, tomato

Desserts: Pumpkin chiffon, lemon flavors, fruits

Fish and Seafood

Appetizers: Relishes, grapefruit, tomato juice, stuffed celery

Potato or substitute: Rice, peas, toast

Vegetables: Tomatoes and okra, green beans, cauliflower, celery, peas, asparagus, spinach, marinated vegetables

Salads: Tomato, cucumber, tossed green, coleslaw, fruit, Caesar, marinated vegetables

Desserts: Angelfood cake, fruit, molded gelatin, lime or lemon flavors

Soups or Meatless

Appetizers: Onion soup, fruit juices, cold cut hors d' oeuvres

Hot Bread: Bread sticks, French bread

Salads or vegetables: Tomatoes, cucumber, orange, tossed green, green beans, coleslaw, gelatin molds, cottage cheese

Desserts: Fruits, angelfood cake, gelatin molds, custard, pudding

Eggs

Appetizers: Fruit juices, stuffed celery, vegetable soup

Potatoes or substitute: Baked or boiled potatoes, toast, peas, corn

Vegetables: Mixed, mushrooms, asparagus, spinach

Salads: Fruit, tomato, raw vegetable

Dessert: Sherbet, fruit, gelatin molds, cookies

Salads

Appetizers: Fruit, tomato soup, cheese, fruit juice

Hot Bread: Bread sticks, French bread

Dessert: Fruit, angelfood cake, custard, pudding

Casseroles

Appetizers: Fruit or fruit juice, consommé, raw vegetables

Salads: Gelatin molds, beets, cucumbers, tomatoes, relishes, tomato aspic, coleslaw, tossed green, fruit.

Desserts: Angelfood cake, fruits, custard, pudding

Pork or Ham

Appetizers: Applesauce, raw vegetables, consommé, fruit, fruit juices

Potato or substitute: Mashed or boiled potatoes, winter squash, sweet potatoes

Vegetables: Broccoli, cabbage, Brussels sprouts, cauliflower, summer squash, beans, okra, spinach, celery, carrots

Salads: Coleslaw, fruit salads or combinations, gelatin molds, cranberry

Dessert: Applesauce, gelatin molds, fruit, baked apples

Shop and Store Foods Wisely

Today's shopper has a wider variety of products to choose from than ever before. Consider the miracle of any given supermarket. Some eight to ten thousand items, packaged in any size, shape and form she may desire are waiting to be plucked from the shelves. Thanks to grades and standards which are rigidly enforced, you can purchase with confidence.

• With your best interests well protected, you need only make a careful selection with your own taste and purpose in mind.

• Shopping for value does not always mean choosing the most expensive. Grades and labels make it safe to **choose the best for your purpose.** The less expensive grades of meat, eggs or fruit are just as nourishing and may serve your purpose better than the top grades. For example, varieties of oranges for squeezing are not necessarily the best for slicing in salads or fruit cups, and vice versa.

• **Shop the newspapers** before you shop the store. Watch for seasonal specials. Fruits, vegetables and meats in abundant supply are, as a rule, better buys.

• Follow the purchasing guides many newspapers run on grocery-ad days or as regular women's page features. **Magazines, radio and TV also are valuable shopping aids.**

• **Shop ahead,** with the meal plans for several days or a full week in mind. Eliminating last-minute trips to the store can save time, money and your good humor.

• **Shop when you have plenty of time** to do an unhurried job, preferably when the store is not crowded.

• **Start with a shopping list** and the resolve to be realistic but be flexible enough to take advantage of good buys. While the temptation is to buy things on impulse, remember that you are likely to trot home with something that doesn't fit into any menu you have planned.

• **Don't let leftovers happen** — intend them. Food items that can be planned for two varied appearances should be bought in quantity accordingly. Buy cuts of meats that can be used for two meals of fresh meat. A large pot-roast can be cut to provide a one-meal pot-roast and enough meat for stew another day. The butcher will cut center slices of ham for one meal, leaving the rest to be baked.

• **Buy only those perishable items you can use promptly.** Even if head lettuce is a real "two-for—" bargain, the savings will be lost if the second head wilts due to lack of adequate storage space or because you cannot use it soon enough.

• **Shop for grade.** Dairy foods, eggs, meats, poultry, some vegetables and canned goods are graded for the consumer. AA and A, No. 1, prime, choice and fancy are top-grade designations. Lower grades are often as desirable for certain uses as top grades.

• **Read the labels** for "restored," "enriched" and "fortified," especially on breads, cereal foods and dairy items. They are well worth their cost in added nutrition. Ingredient listings appear on most packaged and canned products. These can help you buy to satisfy your family's particular taste.

• **Know the quality of the brand you buy.** A less expensive unbranded product may not contain the number of servings or quality you want and may not be the best buy.

BREAKFASTS

If you are a slow starter in the morning, breakfast may not be your favorite meal. If you tend to skip it, though, chances are you're one of the first in line for coffee breaks or are rattling at the cupboards and scanning the refrigerator by 10 or 11 o'clock. Breakfast habits are bound to vary, just as food tastes are. Take a look at yours to see what important foods you are getting. If your only morning energy comes from donuts or sweets at mid-morning, you are probably coming up on the short end of the vitamins and nutrients which your body needs. **Starting the day with a nutritious breakfast is especially important** for children who need lots of energy all day long. Dieters who don't want hunger pangs for several hours before lunchtime finally arrives or who have a hard time controlling a ravenous appetite from lunch until dinner also need morning go-power. If you aren't used to eating breakfast, you may want to develop the habit gradually by starting with juice for awhile. When you're used to that, try some milk along with it. In several weeks your capacity will have developed enough for eggs or cereal.

If time is a problem with breakfast preparation at your house, organize your schedule so that routine details are automatic. Come to the kitchen with the table set, the coffee pot ready to go. Colorful place mats and an attractive table are tempting bait for the potential breakfast skippers in the family.

Night-before preparations can give you a head start in the morning. Prepare and refrigerate fruit or fruit juice, ready to serve. A quick eggnog is a novel way to drink your milk and your egg from the same glass and can be prepared the night before. Or, have ingredients and equipment for making hot cereal or cooking eggs assembled at your fingertips.

The new balanced nutrition drinks, cereals, etc. can be especially valuable help to those who prefer light breakfasts or who have only a short time for preparation. Instant Breakfast made with skim milk contains only 218 calories and contains one fourth of your daily nutritional needs. What a convenience to the dieter! Fortified cereals and other foods can help you deliver breakfast in a hurry and supply your family with many of their needed nutrients.

If breakfast is still a dead end street for you, or if there is no way you can incorporate breakfast into your eating pattern, help yourself to your favorite flavor of Instant Breakfast or other nutritionally balanced food for your coffee break or mid-morning snack. Either has fewer calories than a gooey sweet roll and many more times the nutritional value. The calories will have to be counted, of course, but you'll find that your appetite will be controllable when lunchtime comes.

What should you include in a breakfast? Start with a fruit or fruit juice. Orange, grapefruit, and tomato juices are favorites which everybody knows, but they don't need to be the limit. Discover the variety of juices which are available to you — apricot, cranberry, grape, apple — to mention just a few. Many of the fruit dishes which you can find in the Dessert section of the recipes will make great variations — hot or cold — in your breakfasts.

Include a protein dish, such as eggs, ham, etc., or serve cereal with milk. Such a variety of hot and cold cereals exists on the market today, that you're bound to find several among them that will satisfy both children and adults. Eggs can take center stage on your table in more ways than just boiled, fried or scrambled. Try baking them with cheese on top or baking them in toast cups. You'll find other interesting ideas for fixing eggs in the Main Dish section of the recipes. Favorites, such as French toast, are feasible for the dieter if a high proportion of eggs is used and providing he goes lightly on the syrups or uses fruits as a topping instead. German pancakes and Crepes, both of which are similar to pancakes but have higher proportions of eggs in the batter, are quite nutritious and make great weekend breakfast treats. Instruct the dieters to leave the syrup to those not watching calories and help themselves to fruits that are low in calories and make tasty toppings.

Add a glass of skim milk — plain, chocolate, or any way you like it — especially if you haven't had any with your cereal. If you are a coffee or tea drinker, by all means help yourself to a cup or mugful—watch the sugar and cream, though.

For those who aren't watching calories, you may want to supplement this basic plan with extra helpings or with other things, such as toast, muffins or an occasional sweet roll. You alone know your will power and that of the other dieters, so if you are unable to resist the temptation of such foods sitting in your cupboards, it would be wise on your part to plan on supplementing non-dieters' breakfasts with other, less-tempting foods.

German Pancakes Filled with
   Fruit, page 125
Canadian Bacon, page 86
Coffee or Tea

Top this nutritious pan cake with fresh fruit for a positively plush breakfast, lunch or dessert idea!

GERMAN PANCAKES

   4 eggs
   ⅔ cup flour
   I tablespoon sugar
   ½ teaspoon salt
   ⅔ cup skim milk
   2 tablespoons cooking oil

OVEN 400°   4 SERVINGS
                             234 Calories Each

Grease two 9-inch round pans. In medium mixing bowl, beat eggs slightly. Add remaining ingredients; mix well. Pour batter into pans. Bake at 400° for 20 minutes. Reduce heat to 350°; continue baking for 10 minutes. Slide onto plates. Serve with fruit.

Tip: To make in blender, process eggs on low speed until light yellow in color. Add remaining ingredients; process on medium speed until blended. Bake as directed.

CANADIAN-STYLE BACON

                 33 Calories Per ⅛-Inch Thick Slice

Place bacon in large cold frypan. Heat slowly, separating slices so that they lie flat in fry pan. Fry slowly 2 to 3 minutes. Turn slices and fry 2 to 3 minutes longer until bacon is well-done. Drain on paper towel.

Try some of these ideas for convenient week-day breakfasts:

Cranberry Juice	81
Hot Cereal with Milk	170
Coffee or Tea	00
Total	251
Mapled Peaches, page 131	89
Cold Cereal with Skim Milk	165
Coffee or Tea	00
Total	254
Melon Cantaloupe Slice	60
Scrambled Eggs, page 99	178
Skim Milk	90
Coffee or Tea	00
Total	328
French Toast with Fresh Berries	390
Skim Milk	90
Coffee or Tea	00
Total	480
Orange Juice or Slices	110
Eggs Baked in Toast Cups, page 96	190
Skim Milk	90
Coffee or Tea	00
Total	390
Instant Breakfast	218
Coffee or Tea	00
Total	218
Spicy Fruit, page 130	183
Baked Custard, page 125	140
Toast	60
Coffee or Tea	00
Total	383
Eggnog, page 57	158
Toast	60
Coffee or Tea	00
Total	218
Fruit Platter	200
Toast	60
Skim Milk	90
Coffee or Tea	00
Total	350

Weekend breakfasts give you a chance to try new and interesting breakfast ideas. Enjoy a leisurely Sunday breakfast of:

Crepes Topped with Peach Slices or Berries, page 126	310
Skim Milk	90
Coffee or Tea	00
Total	400

Or, combine breakfast and lunch into a lazy-day brunch.

Orange-Grapefruit Juice	84
Spanish Omelet, page 95	190
Toast	60
Coffee or Tea	00
Total	334
German Pancakes Filled with Fruit, page 125	300
Canadian Bacon, page 86	66
Coffee or Tea	00
Total	366

LUNCHES

Lunches are the mid-day breaks for refueling, relaxing and refreshing. If they become hurried affairs, grabbed on the run, they defeat their purpose. Wherever you are, at home, school, office or restaurant, **take time to sit down, to enjoy the food you're eating, to take a breather from whatever occupied the morning and to restore your mental and physical energies for the afternoon's activities.** Even if you eat lunch at home by yourself or with small children, lunch can be a time to relax, rather than several minutes to stash away some quick, high-calorie, low-nutrition snacks before rushing frazzled, through the remainder of the afternoon.

Depending on the number of calories you have alloted for lunch, assemble some sensible foods for your appetite pleasure. A good lunch can include a main dish (soup, main dish salad, meat, open-faced sandwich, etc.), a vegetable or a fruit for dessert, and a glass of milk or other beverage. Preparation doesn't have to be time-consuming. Let your lunch be inspired by a recent dinner menu — a chance to bring off a quick trick with leftovers, or try one of our recipes for quick soups, salads, or main dishes. Give a little thought to what you intend to have for lunch before you start eating it. This will give you time to relax, reducing the part of hunger that stems from anxiety, and can help you to **get the most taste from your food when you do sit down to eat.** Milk can appear in other than the traditional glass form. Try it in a nutritious custard or pudding, or use it in preparing a healthful eggnog.

If you just can't take a half hour in your schedule for lunch, sip slowly on a cold, frosty glass of Instant Breakfast made with skim milk for the ten minutes that you can spare. Layer your open-faced sandwich (made with lower calorie spreads) with the lettuce or other fingerable food on top, so that you can carry it with you in the car as you run your errands. Assemble your salad plate or prepare your lunch ahead of time — perhaps at breakfast — so that it's ready-to-go when lunch-time rolls around. However, if you decide to compensate for your busy schedule, **don't let lack of time be your excuse for indulging in excess calories** for which you will be sorry later.

On the following pages you'll find some ideas for lunch combinations, lunch-box suggestions, and week-end lunches. Use similar foods from the same food groups with comparable calorie counts to substitute in these menus and provide endless variety. For those of you who must eat in restaurants at lunch-time, page 10 will give you some good suggestions on how to eat out successfully without massacring your diet.

Open-Faced Bologna Sandwich	340
Raw Cauliflowerettes	26
Dill Pickle	15
Skim Milk	90
Grapes	50
Total	521

Snazz up the lunches you pack with napkins of brilliant colors or wild patterns. Lunch bags not only come in the traditional brown color, but are also available in yellow, pink, blue and green. A simple drawing made with magic marker can personalize a small child's lunch and make low calorie sack lunches a real treat. For your teenager who is on a diet and carries his lunch, tuck in a package of unshelled sunflower seeds. They're quite low in calories and will take a large portion of the lunch hour to shell and eat. Send your dieting husband off to work with an interesting lunch packed in his brief case or lunch box. Include a cartoon, joke, or personal note as a surprise, or pack in one of his favorite cigars for a low calorie dessert. Something out of the ordinary — whether it's food or a surprise — takes the monotony out of sack lunches and can encourage the dieter.

Open-faced sandwiches reduce the calories by one piece of bread. Cut them in half; fold together and store in plastic wrap for low caloried convenience.

Try some of these garnishes to make a sandwich unusual: sliced dill pickle, thin slices of onion ,radish slices, green pepper rings, different varieties of lettuces.

Use mustard or other low calorie spreads on your bread. Salad dressing contains fewer calories than mayonnaise but should still be used sparingly.

To prevent soggy bread, moist sandwich ingredients can be wrapped separately and added by the luncher before he eats the sandwich.

Cut sandwiches into halves or quarters; it seems like you're eating more if there are more pieces.

Moist foods, such as pickles, canned fruits, etc., travel well in plastic bags tied tightly at the top.

Chicken and meat sandwiches can be made ahead and frozen. Make a week's supply at one time. Wrap individually and label according to type.

Pack crushable fruit or raw vegetables in paper cups or other crush-proof container so that the food arrives at lunchtime in prime condition.

Raw vegetables — carrots, celery, cauliflower, turnips, radishes, etc.—give a crunch to lunches, add nutrition and pack very easily.

Hard boiled eggs are easy to eat; pack tiny salt and pepper shakers with them. Or, turn them into deviled eggs and place two halves together before wrapping.

Lots of good things can be carried in a wide mouth vacuum jar — hot soup, chilled canned fruits, special beverages, etc.

Tuna Asparagus Salad 309
Whole Wheat Bread 55
Skim Milk 90
Mandarin Orange Slices 55

Total 509

For weekends, or other days that several people are home, you may want to try some more hearty menus including: main dish salads, hearty soups, easy-to-prepare main dishes or favorite sandwiches. Fix the low calorie meal with the dieter in mind, and add onto it as needed for the rest of the crowd.

Here are some easy suggestions for lunches at home during the week:

Old Fashioned Vegetable Soup
page 63 101
Slice Cheddar Cheese.......... 112
Apple 70
Coffee or Tea 00

Total 283

Open-Faced Bologna Sandwich .. 190
Orange 73
Skim Milk 90

Total 353

Hard-Cooked Egg 78
Tossed Salad with Vinegar
Dressing 20
Skim Milk 90
Grapes 40

Total 228

Fruit Platter 200
Cottage Cheese 60
Toast 60
Coffee 00

Total 320

Tuna Stuffed Tomato, page 119 ... 138
Toast or Bread 60
Skim Milk 90

Total 288

Wiener 155
Kraut Salad, page 119 67
Skim Milk 90
Grapes 40

Total 352

Bouillon Sipper, page 47 30
Chef's Salad, page 115 332
Skim Milk 90

Total 452

Beef Consommé 30
Roast Beef Slice 302
Lettuce Salad with Vinegar
Dressing 20
Coffee or Tea 00
Peach 35

Total 387

Cold Cuts 146
Creamy Coleslaw, page 120 91
Coffee or Tea 00
Orange 73

Total 310

Meatloaf, page 76 239
Carrot Sticks 20
Skim Milk 90

Total 349

Fish Creole, page 41 203
Relishes 30
Skim Milk 90

Total 323

Open-Faced Chicken Sandwich .. 210
Dilled Onion Rings, page 61 55
Skim Milk 90
Cantaloupe 60

Total 415

DINNER

Unless your family has the fortune of having similar departing times in the morning so that you can eat breakfast together, dinner is probably the only meal at which every member is present and accounted for. So, most likely you put in some special efforts for dinner that you can't for other meals. Because you want to make the most of the time that the family is together, dinner deserves careful planning, with an eye not only to nutrition, but also to pleasure and enjoyment. **Healthful food and pleasant feelings create a warm family atmosphere.**

The week's meal planning is most often based on the main dishes served at dinner. These provide clues for the most congenial vegetables, salads and desserts to serve with them. They also provide opportunity to build into your planning wise uses of leftovers for other main dishes or for lunches on subsequent days. Dinners planned according to your family's needs of the basic four food groups fall into an easy pattern that allows you to include their favorite foods, as well as introduce new foods from time to time.

Start by selecting your main dish. If you **plan several menus together, you can make economical use of leftovers** and avoid needless last minute trips to the store for ingredients you don't have on hand.

On the next several pages you'll find ideas for various types of evening meals — company and guest menus, family suppers, family special occasions and budget-wise meals. Following the basic guide of combining two vegetables (or one vegetable and one salad) with a main dish and adding a dessert to complete the meal, we've also given suggestions on how you can expand these menus to satisfy those at your table who are not weight conscious. If we've suggested dishes which your family has not yet learned to appreciate, substitute something you would prefer instead of it. The go-together chart, page 32, gives you some ideas on combinations we like; you may find these useful. But don't hesitate to incorporate your own and your family's thinking into your dinner menus.

Steak Dinner in Foil 310
Relishes 50
Coffee or Tea 0
Raspberry Peach Freeze 104

Total....479

What a convenient family dinner! Make the refreshing frozen fruit dessert earlier in the day. Wrap round steak, potatoes, carrots and beans in foil to bake by themselves into a delicious meal. Prepare your relish tray; cover it and let it chill in the refrigerator (while you help the children with their homework) until this carefree dinner is ready. Hearty and light flavors, soft and crisp textures, and refreshing colors are the keys to this convenience meal.

Your entire dinner is baked in the oven! Serve it with a wedge of lettuce for a very easily prepared meal.

STEAK DINNER IN FOIL

2 lbs. round steak
1 tablespoon (3 teaspoons) salt or seasoned salt
2 teaspoons MSG (monosodium glutamate), if desired
Dash pepper
4 cups (6 small) peeled and quartered potatoes
3 cups (6 med.) peeled carrot pieces
1¾ cups (10-oz. pkg.) frozen green beans

OVEN 350°   6 SERVINGS
                             310 Calories Each

Trim fat from meat. Sprinkle steak with 2 teaspoons of the salt, MSG and pepper. Place meat in center of a piece of heavy duty foil. Place potatoes and carrots on top of steak. Sprinkle with remaining 1 teaspoon of the salt. Bring edges of foil together and seal with a double fold. Place seam side up in a shallow baking pan. Bake at 350° for 1 hour. Remove from oven; unwrap. Place frozen beans on top of carrots. Reseal; continue baking 45 minutes until steak and beans are tender.

Smooth and frothy, this colorful frozen dessert is bound to be a pleaser. Fresh tasting with frozen raspberries. Make ahead — about 5 hours.

RASPBERRY-PEACH FREEZE

- 1¼ cups (10-oz. pkg.) thawed and undrained frozen raspberries
- 1 tablespoon (1 envelope) unflavored gelatin
- 1 cup (8-oz. can) undrained peach slices*
- 1 tablespoon unsweetened lemon juice
- ⅓ cup sugar
- ¼ cup instant nonfat dry milk
- ¼ cup ice water**
- 2 egg whites

8 (½ cup) SERVINGS
104 Calories Each

In medium saucepan, heat raspberries and gelatin over medium heat, stirring until gelatin is dissolved. Add peaches, lemon juice and sugar. Chill until slightly thickened. In small mixer bowl, beat nonfat dry milk, ice water and egg whites until stiff peaks form. Fold into fruit mixture. Pour into 8 or 9-inch square pan or ice cube tray. Freeze until firm, about 4 to 5 hours. For ease in serving, remove from freezer 10 minutes before serving.

Tips: *An 8-oz. can undrained peach slices equals ¾ cup peach slices and ⅓ cup liquid.

**Place a few ice cubes in water until ice cold; this is essential for proper whipping.

39

Make this meal in the oven. Fish creole features a tomatoey sauce; the mild flavor of baked potatoes adds white and brown; and green beans round out the flavor and highlight the color with green. This is an easy dinner to do. Put the fish and potato in the oven. Prepare the melon balls; and while those chill, put the beans in to cook. Then, relax and take the last half hour before dinner to enjoy with your husband and family.

Haddock, cod or halibut fillets, baked with a creole-type sauce.

FISH CREOLE

I lb. haddock, cod or halibut fillets, thawed
I tablespoon butter or margarine
I cup (8 oz. can) stewed tomatoes, cut into pieces
¼ cup (½ med.) chopped onion or
   I tablespoon instant minced onion
¼ cup finely chopped celery
 2 tablespoons chopped green pepper
¼ cup sugar
½ teaspoon salt
¼ teaspoon leaf oregano, if desired
⅛ teaspoon pepper

OVEN 350°   4 SERVINGS
                       203 Calories Each

Rinse the fish fillets and dry with a towel. Arrange in 9-inch square or IIx7-inch pan. In medium saucepan, melt butter. Stir in remaining ingredients; mix well. Carefully pour tomato mixture over fish fillets. Bake at 350° for 40 to 50 minutes until fish flakes.

Cool, refreshing cantaloupe with a taste of lime to make a sensational flavor combination. Serve in melon shell for added interest as an appetizer, salad or dessert.

TANGY MELON BALLS

3 cups (I med.) cantaloupe balls*
2 tablespoons lime or lemon juice

                      6 (½ cup) SERVINGS
                       37 Calories Each

In large mixing bowl, combine cantaloupe and lime juice. Mix well. Chill I to 2 hours before serving. If desired, garnish with a slice of lime or lemon.

Tip: *Frozen melon balls can be used for the fresh. Honeydew melon tastes terrific prepared like this, too.

OVEN BAKED GREEN BEANS

1¾ cups (10-oz. pkg.) frozen cut green beans
 2 tablespoons water
¼ teaspoon salt

OVEN 350°   4 SERVINGS
                       19 Calories Each

Place beans in ungreased I to 1½-quart casserole or baking dish. Top with water and salt. Bake, covered, at 350° for 45 to 60 minutes until tender.

Delight your family with this colorful main dish that can be prepared on your barbecue or in your broiler. Since the main dish contains meat and vegetables, all you need to add is a lettuce wedge and bread. The lettuce gives a crispness to your meal, and the salad dressing with it provides not only a creamy texture but also a tangy flavor contrast. The crunch and color contrast of French bread tops off the combination. After a meal with foods that have definite flavors, such as this, enjoy a mildly flavored, custardy dessert.

What could be more colorful, nutritious and fun than this meat-vegetable combination. An ideal summer treat from the grill, too! Try the shrimp variation. Allow time to marinate.

MEAT-VEGETABLE KABOBS

    2 lbs. sirloin steak, 1-inch thick
       (cut into 1x1-inch pieces)
    2 cups (1 pt.) cherry tomatoes
    2 cups (1 pt.) fresh mushrooms
    1 large green pepper, cut into 1½-inch
       square pieces
    ½ cup wine or cider vinegar
    2 tablespoons cooking oil
    1 teaspoon instant minced onion
    2 tablespoons sugar
    ½ teaspoon garlic salt
    ¼ teaspoon salt
    ¼ teaspoon leaf oregano

BROIL   8 SKEWERS
                                    175 Calories Each

Place meat cubes, tomatoes, mushrooms and green pepper in a shallow baking dish. Combine remaining ingredients; mix well and pour over meat and vegetables. Cover; marinate several hours at room temperature or overnight in refrigerator, turning occasionally. Arrange meat and vegetables on 8 long skewers. Drain. Place on broiling pan; broil 4 to 6 inches from heat for about 5 minutes, turning occasionally for even browning. (Additional brushings with marinade will add extra calories.)

Tips: For Shrimp-Vegetable Kabobs, 3½ cups fresh or frozen shrimp (about 12-oz. pkg.), cleaned and thawed, can be used for the meat cubes. Broil until shrimp begins to turn white and vegetables are tender.

To grill over coals, place kabobs on rack 6 inches above hot coals and grill 5 to 7 minutes, turning occasionally for even browning.

If well done meat or more crisp vegetables are desired, place meat on skewer first and broil or grill until almost done. Then place vegetables on end of skewer and continue until done.

SEASONED FRENCH BREAD

    ¼ cup butter or margarine, melted
    1 teaspoon garlic salad dressing mix or
       garlic salt*
    8 1-inch slices French bread

OVEN 350°   8 SLICES
                                    110 Calories Each

Combine butter and salad dressing mix. Spread on French bread. Wrap tightly in foil; bake at 350° for 15 minutes until heated through. Serve hot.

Tips: *Other salad dressing mixes can be used for the garlic. We especially like Italian and French.

To broil French bread, place 2 to 3 inches from heat for 2 to 3 minutes until brown.

This apricot flavored dessert bakes to form two layers. Turn this nutritious dessert upside-down when cool to serve, and enjoy a creamy custard over a sponge-type cake.

SPUN GOLD DESSERT

    3 eggs
    ½ teaspoon salt
    ½ cup sugar
    1½ cups (12-oz. can) apricot nectar
    1 tablespoon lemon juice
    1 tablespoon butter or margarine, melted
    ¼ cup flour

OVEN 325°   8 (¾ cup) SERVINGS
                                    129 Calories Each

Generously grease 8 6-oz. custard cups. Separate eggs, placing whites in large mixer bowl; yolks in small mixer bowl. Add salt to egg whites; beat until soft peaks form. Gradually beat in ¼ cup of sugar until stiff peaks form; set aside. Using same beaters, combine egg yolks, apricot nectar, lemon juice, butter, flour and remaining ¼ cup of sugar. Beat until smooth. By hand, fold into egg white mixture until thoroughly combined. Fill custard cups to ¼-inch from top. Place in large shallow baking pan. Pour hot water in pan around cups until about 1-inch deep. Bake at 325° for 45 to 55 minutes until knife inserted in center comes out clean. Cool enough to handle; invert onto plates to serve. Or, chill and invert to serve.

Tip: For those not watching calories, 1 teaspoon apricot jam can be placed in the bottom of each cup before filling, if desired. Or, serve with whipped cream or whipped topping, if desired.

                    Total 362

For the night that you have only 30 minutes left to prepare dinner, these easy dishes save the day for you and are sure to score with your family. Weiners in a barbecue-like sauce, the cool crispness of coleslaw, and a favorite vegetable satisfy your family attractively and nutritiously. Serve them milk and a quick apple dessert to complete their nutritional needs, and you've done it again, Mom!

Wieners in a spicy barbecue sauce. These will be a favorite treat for your children. Easy to make on a hurried evening.

SNAPPY WIENERS

¾ lb. (6) wieners
1½ tablespoons catsup
1 tablespoon cider vinegar
1 tablespoon instant minced onion or
¼ cup (½ med.) chopped onion
2 teaspoons Worcestershire sauce
¾ teaspoon horseradish, 1 tablespoon prepared mustard or 1 teaspoon dry mustard

OVEN 350°   6 SERVINGS
                                    133 Calories Each

Score wieners diagonally. Place in ungreased 1½-quart baking dish. In small mixing bowl, combine remaining ingredients; mix well. Pour over wieners. Bake, covered, at 350° for 30 minutes. Serve hot.

Tip: To prepare in saucepan, heat over medium heat for 10 to 15 minutes until heated through.

Tart coleslaw in vinegar dressing. Serve it to your family in only 20 minutes!

BASIC TANGY COLESLAW

3 cups (½ med. head) cabbage, shredded or thinly sliced
¼ cup sliced green onion
¼ cup chopped parsley, if desired
1 tablespoon sugar
2 tablespoons vinegar

                          6 (½ cup) SERVINGS
                              25 Calories Each

In large mixing bowl, combine all ingredients; toss lightly. Serve immediately.

Tips: For a crisp chilled coleslaw, shredded cabbage can be chilled in ice water for about an hour. Drain and combine with remaining ingredients.

For Caraway Slaw, add ¼ cup sliced radishes and ½ teaspoon caraway seed to cabbage mixture.

For Vegetable Slaw, add 2 carrots, sliced, ½ cup sliced radishes and 1 medium stalk celery, sliced, to cabbage mixture.

Leftover servings can be stored, covered, in refrigerator for several days.

Marshmallows melt into the apples and make a very yummy topping. So easy and quick, you'll keep this one as a stand-by.

IMPROMPTU APPLES

4 cups (4 med.) peeled and thinly sliced apples
Dash cinnamon, allspice or cloves
8 marshmallows, cut in half

OVEN 350°   6 (½ cup) SERVINGS
                                91 Calories Each

In ungreased 9x5-inch loaf pan or baking dish, arrange apple slices. Sprinkle with cinnamon. Top with marshmallow halves. Bake, covered, at 350° for 45 to 50 minutes until apples are tender. Serve hot.

Tip: For those not watching calories, drizzle with cream or top with ice cream before serving, if desired.

For that special family occasion or the evening your husband's boss comes for dinner, here's a type of dinner you can serve. Appetize them with a clear bouillon sipper. Then, bring on the luscious brown lambs steaks, juicy golden corn and a crisp, green spinach salad. If you suspect the guests to be heavy eaters, serve a dinner roll to them, too. Relax and chat over your coffee and refreshing fruit dessert. You've got an elegant dinner — very satisfying, yet won't obliterate your calorie counting efforts.

BOUILLON SIPPER

2¾ cups (two 10½-oz. cans) condensed beef
   bouillon
1 cup hot water
2 to 3 tablespoons sherry, if desired

6 SERVINGS
30 Calories Each

In medium saucepan, combine beef bouillon, water and sherry. Heat through. Serve hot in mugs, topped with lemon slices and parsley.

BROILED LAMB STEAKS

192 Calories Per ¼ LB.

Set regulator to broil. Place lamb steaks on broiler rack. Insert broiler pan and rack so the top of 1-inch steaks is 2-inches from the heat. When one side is browned, season with salt and pepper; turn and finish cooking on second side. (One-inch steaks require 10 to 12 minutes total cooking time.)

Other Seasonings for Lamb Steaks: Add a dash of garlic salt, paprika or curry powder when seasoning with salt and pepper.

SPINACH AND BACON TOSS

4 strips bacon, crumbled
¼ cup vinegar
2 tablespoons water
1 tablespoon sugar
½ teaspoon salt
¼ teaspoon pepper
8 cups fresh spinach leaves, torn into
   bite-size pieces

6 (1 cup) SERVINGS
61 Calories Each

Fry bacon until crisp; drain and crumble. Mix vinegar, water, sugar, salt and pepper with crumbled bacon. Pour mixture over spinach; toss lightly. Serve immediately.

Add zip to your corn on the cob. Just baste with dry onion soup mixed with water and salt. Yum! Try on barbecue grill, too!

ONION CORN ON THE COB

1 envelope (1¼-oz. pkg.) onion soup mix
½ cup water
½ teaspoon salt
8 ears corn

OVEN 425°

8 SERVINGS
117 Calories Each

In small mixing bowl, combine onion soup mix, water and salt; mix well. Place each ear on piece of foil. Spread each ear of corn with 1 tablespoon onion soup mixture. Wrap ears tightly in foil. Bake at 425° for 30 to 35 minutes until tender.

Tip: Wrapped ears of corn can be placed on grill over hot coals. Cook as directed.

FRUIT A-BOBS

¼ cup orange juice
¼ cup lemon juice
¼ cup sugar
2 cups fresh strawberries
2 cups purple grapes, halved and seeds
   removed
2 medium bananas, cut in ¾-inch slices
2 cups (½ melon) cantaloupe balls
16 skewers

8 SERVINGS
105 Calories Each

Blend juices and sugar. Pour over mixed fruit and chill. Alternate berries, melon balls and other fruit on skewers. Just before serving, stick kabobs into large apple, orange, grapefruit or melon.

Tip: For those not watching calories, serve with Lemon Dip.

Lemon Dip:

1 cup plain yogurt
3 tablespoons powdered sugar
½ teaspoon grated lemon peel

1 CUP DIP
16 Calories Per Tablespoon

Combine all ingredients.

Entertaining is easy when you make the sauces, salad and dessert ahead of time and let the guests do their own cooking. The hearty flavor of vegetables and meat is contrasted by a zesty orange salad on lettuce. Serve rice as a natural go-together for Oriental food, and finish with a lovely chocolate flourish. The congenial company of friends you enjoy and this conversation-sparkling meal combine to make a wonderful evening for both you and your guests. What a great opportunity to play on a foreign theme for a centerpiece and other decorations you may want.

MANDARIN SALAD

>   3 cups (2 II-oz. cans) drained mandarin
>   oranges
>   I cup (2 stalks) sliced celery
> ¼ cup flaked coconut
>   I tablespoon sugar
>   2 tablespoons plain yogurt

6 (⅔ cup) SERVINGS
75 Calories Each

In medium mixing bowl, combine oranges celery and coconut; toss lightly. Add sugar and yogurt; toss gently until well blended. Chill until serving time. Serve on crisp lettuce.

48

Use your fondue pot for cooking this typical Chinese dish. Arrange the meats, fish and vegetables on a pretty tray; then, let each guest cook his own in the hot chicken broth.

CHINESE HOT POT FONDUE

- **2 chicken breasts, skinned, boned and cut into thin strips, page 79**
- **½ lb. boneless beef sirloin, cut into thin strips**
- **1½ cups (7 oz.) fresh or frozen* shrimp**
- **2 cups fresh spinach or sliced Chinese cabbage**
- **2 cups (8 oz. or 1 pt.) fresh mushrooms**
- **½ head cauliflower divided into small pieces**
- **6 cups chicken broth****
- **2 teaspoons salt**

4 SERVINGS
208 Calories Each

Prepare chicken, beef, shrimp and vegetables; arrange on serving tray. Cover and refrigerate until time to serve. Prepare desired sauces. (Use bottled soy sauce, sweet and sour sauce, mustard sauce, teriyaki sauce or prepare your own — see recipes that follow.) Heat chicken broth and salt until bubbly. Pour into fondue pot; place over heating unit in center of table. Set out dishes of sauces. Each guest uses fondue fork to spear piece of vegetable and/or meat and cooks it in the hot chicken broth. Serve with rice (use a covered dish or warming tray to keep warm throughout meal) and sauces. From time to time, spoon some of chicken broth over rice or pass additional broth.

Tips: *Frozen shrimp can be just thawed and set out; however, they lack the pretty pink color. For more attractive shrimp, dip into boiling water just until pink and firm.

**For chicken broth, use broth from stewed chicken or the canned chicken broth — use enough to fill fondue pot about ⅔ full. If desired, use 1 cup white wine or sherry for 1 cup of chicken broth.

If desired, ½ lb. lamb, cut into thin strips, and 1 eggplant, cut into ½-inch cubes, can be used for the beef and cauliflower.

TERIYAKI SAUCE:

½ CUP SAUCE
18 Calories Per Tablespoon

In small saucepan, combine 2 teaspoons cornstarch with 1 teaspoon ground ginger, ¼ cup white wine and ¼ cup soy sauce. Cook over medium heat, stirring constantly, until thickened; serve warm.

CREAMY MUSTARD SAUCE:

½ CUP SAUCE
10 Calories Per Tablespoon

Combine ½ cup plain yogurt with 1½ tablespoons prepared mustard and a few drops of Tabasco sauce. Refrigerate until served.

SWEET AND SOUR SAUCE:

1 CUP SAUCE
43 Calories Per Tablespoon

In small saucepan, combine ½ cup firmly packed brown sugar with 1 tablespoon cornstarch, ½ teaspoon salt, ½ teaspoon paprika, ½ cup pineapple juice and ¼ cup vinegar. Cook over medium heat, stirring constantly, until thickened; serve warm.

A delicate chocolate dessert, velvety and fluffy — that will melt in your mouth. For those not watching calories, top with whipped topping. Or, set into a crust for a chocolate cream pie.

MOCK CHOCOLATE MOUSSE

- **1 tablespoon (1 envelope) unflavored gelatin**
- **2 cups skim milk**
- **1 tablespoon cornstarch**
- **¼ cup sugar**
- **1 egg, separated**
- **⅓ cup semi-sweet chocolate pieces**
- **1 teaspoon vanilla**
- **¼ cup instant nonfat dry milk**
- **¼ cup ice water***

8 (½ cup) SERVINGS
106 Calories Each

Chill small mixer bowl and beaters in refrigerator. In medium saucepan, soften gelatin in ½ cup of the skim milk. To the softened gelatin, add cornstarch, sugar, remaining 1½ cups skim milk, egg yolk and chocolate pieces. Cook over medium heat, stirring constantly, until mixture begins to thicken and comes to a boil. Remove from heat. Stir in vanilla. Chill until slightly thickened but not set. In small, chilled mixer bowl, beat nonfat dry milk, ice water and egg white at high speed until stiff peaks form. Fold into chocolate mixture. Carefully pour into serving dishes. Chill about 2 hours until firm.

Tip: *Place a few ice cubes in water until ice cold; this is essential for proper whipping.

Leftover beef takes on a brand new look in this nutritious stew. Make earlier in the day and reheat before dinner or start preparing it one hour in advance.

HURRY BEEF STEW

    2 cups (4 med.) cut-up carrot (1½-inch pieces)
    2 cups (4 stalks) cut-up celery (1½-inch pieces)
  1½ cups (½ lb.) cubed cooked lean beef
  1½ cups water
    I cup tomato juice*
    I cup (2 small) quartered turnips
    I medium onion, quartered
    I teaspoon salt
    ½ teaspoon garlic salt or ¼ teaspoon instant minced garlic
    ⅛ to ¼ teaspoon pepper
    I bay leaf
    I bouillon cube or I teaspoon instant bouillon

4 (1⅓ cups) SERVINGS
171 Calories

In large saucepan, combine all ingredients. Bring to a boil. Reduce heat; simmer, covered, for 45 to 60 minutes until vegetables are tender and flavors well blended. Remove bay leaf. Serve hot.

Tips: *For a flavor variation, use ½ cup tomato juice and ½ cup red wine for the I cup tomato juice.

To thicken juices, combine 2 tablespoons flour with ¼ cup cold water; mix thoroughly. Drizzle over stew; stir very gently until sauce thickens. Serve with sauce.

Try a budget meal in which the main dish features leftover beef. The vegetables and meat in the stew give you soft and chewy textures, as well as color variety. Carry it several steps further and add tartness and crispness with marinated cauliflower served on lettuce leaves. A glass of skim milk balances the nutrition, and a cool, frothy gelatin dessert ends this hearty meal with a gentle touch.

Light and lovely — this dessert is a treat to the dieter and the non-dieter. Make earlier in the afternoon so it will have time to chill.

Cauliflower marinated in your choice of dressing. An interesting salad — easy when made ahead and mellowed in refrigerator. We suggest you use white vinegar for the best appearance.

CAULIFLOWER SALAD

1¾ cups (10-oz. pkg.) thawed frozen cauliflower
1 tablespoon sliced green onion or chopped chives
1 tablespoon capers, if desired
¼ cup low calorie salad dressing of your choice*
¼ head lettuce

6 SERVINGS
52 Calories Each**

In medium mixing bowl, combine all ingredients except lettuce. Cover and chill 2 to 3 hours. Just before serving, tear lettuce into bite-size pieces and place in salad bowl. Add cauliflower mixture; toss lightly. Serve immediately.

Tips: *We especially like Italian Dressing or Old Fashioned French Dressing on this salad.

**Calories have been calculated using French Dressing, page 123. Other salad dressings will differ in calories.

If desired, 1 small head fresh cauliflower can be used for the frozen. Separate into cauliflowerettes (cauliflower does not need to be cooked). Prepare as directed.

For those not watching calories, garnish with sliced pitted ripe olives, if desired.

LIME CHIFFON

1 package (3 oz.) lime flavored gelatin
1 cup boiling water
1 cup cold water
1 egg white
1 teaspoon finely grated lime peel, if desired

4 (1 cup) SERVINGS
85 Calories Each

In small mixing bowl, dissolve gelatin in boiling water. Add cold water; mix well. Chill until slightly thickened but not set. In small mixer bowl, beat egg white on high speed until soft peaks form. Add gelatin mixture, beating constantly until thick and foamy. Chill 2 hours until set.

Tips: For Pineapple Lime Chiffon, fold ½ cup drained crushed pineapple into foamy mixture before chilling.

For those not watching calories, garnish with whipped topping.

Cornish Hens with
   Wild Rice Stuffing 350
Broccoli with Zesty Cheese Sauce 41
Cranberry Mold 199
Coffee, Tea 0
Fruit Fondue 85
                            Total....675

Having special guests for dinner? Cornish hens, with a wild rice and pineapple stuffing, are just the thing to serve them royally. Pineapple adds a light refreshing touch to the hearty stuffing; and a cranberry gelatin mold adds not only color and flavor interest, but also lends a crunch from the celery in it. Round out the color with broccoli and the textures with a zippy cheese sauce. If your guests are known to be especially hearty eaters, you may want to add rolls for them, too.

Bring everyone into the picture with a do-it-yourself dessert. Fruit Fondue lets everyone dip their own fruit into an orangey sauce — a great, relaxing way to end a meal. Flavors leave you refreshed, too. A wonderful, reduced calorie dinner that lets you stay on your diet, yet is complete and attractive enough to please any guests you're entertaining.

CORNISH GAME HENS WITH PINEAPPLE-WILD RICE STUFFING

4 Rock Cornish game hens
1 tablespoon butter or margarine
½ cup (1 med.) chopped onion
¼ cup chopped green pepper
3 cups cooked wild rice
3 cups cooked rice
1 cup drained crushed pineapple
1½ teaspoons salt
¼ teaspoon pepper

OVEN 325°   8 SERVINGS
                        350 Calories Each

Lightly sprinkle cavity of hens with salt.
In large fry pan, sauté mushrooms, onion and green pepper in butter. Add wild rice, rice, pineapple, salt and pepper. Toss lightly. Stuff hens. Fasten with skewers or wooden picks. Place breast sides up on rack in roasting pan. Do not cover. Bake at 325° for 1 hour. Cover and bake one hour longer until tender. Cut hens in half and serve with stuffing.

Use this basic Cream Sauce as a reduced calorie base for your favorite sauces. Note tips for some variations we suggest.

CREAM SAUCE

    2 tablespoons flour
    2 tablespoons instant nonfat dry milk
    I teaspoon seasoned salt or salt
    ½ teaspoon MSG (monosodium glutamate),
      if desired
    ¼ teaspoon salt
      Dash pepper
    I¼ cups cold water

I¼ CUPS SAUCE
4 Calories Per Tablespoon

In small saucepan, combine all ingredients except water; mix well. Add water slowly, stirring well. Cook over medium heat, stirring constantly, until mixture thickens and comes to a boil. Serve.

Tips: For Creamy Gravy, I to 4 tablespoons meat juices or ½ teaspoon Kitchen Bouquet can be added after the water.

For extra flavor, I bouillon cube, dissolved in ¼ cup hot water, can be added after the water; omit salt and reduce water to I cup.

To use skim milk, add I¼ cups skim milk to flour mixture; omit instant nonfat dry milk and water.

For Zesty Cheese Sauce, use regular salt; add ¼ cup grated Cheddar or American cheese and dash Worcestershire sauce to thickened mixture. Stir until cheese is melted.

Leftovers can be stored, covered, in refrigerator for about I week. Reheat for reuse.

CRANBERRY MOLD

    I package (3 oz.) raspberry flavored gelatin
    ¾ cup boiling water
    2 cups (I-lb. can) whole cranberry sauce
    ½ cup (I stalk) sliced celery
    I tablespoon fresh grated orange peel or
    2 tablespoons prepared orange peel

5 (½ cup) SERVINGS
199 Calories Each

In small mixing bowl, dissolve gelatin in boiling water. Mix in cranberry sauce, celery and orange peel; stir until dissolved. Pour into 3 to 4-cup mold. Chill about 2 hours until firm.

"Dress up" fruits with this citrus-flavored sauce — either use as a dip or serve over desserts as a topping.

FRUIT FONDUE

    I tablespoon cornstarch
    I cup orange juice
    I tablespoon unsweetened lemon juice
    2 tablespoons sugar
      Fresh or canned friuts such as straw-
      berries, green grapes or banana slices

I CUP SAUCE
15 Calories Per Tablespoon

In small saucepan, combine all ingredients. Cook over medium heat, stirring constantly, until mixture thickens and comes to a boil. Serve warm with a selection of your favorite fresh or canned fruits. Stir occasionally.

Tip: This sauce can be served warm or cold as a topping on other desserts.

Beverages, Snacks & Soups

Please your guests with this hot, spicy beverage.

HOLIDAY WASSAIL BOWL

    6 cups apple juice
    2 cups cranberry juice cocktail
    ½ cup orange juice
    3 cinnamon sticks, broken
    I teaspoon whole allspice
    ½ teaspoon whole cloves
    I teaspoon aromatic bitters, if desired
       Clove-studded orange slices, if desired

17 (½ cup) SERVINGS
63 Calories Each

In large saucepan, combine apple juice, cranberry juice and orange juice. Tie cinnamon sticks, allspice and cloves in porous cloth; add to liquid. Heat to boiling; simmer 10 minutes. Remove from heat. Let stand 10 more minutes. Remove spice bag; add bitters. Pour into punch bowl. Garnish with clove-studded orange slices. Serve hot.

Tips: This can be made very nicely in an electric saucepan. Easy to serve from and to keep warm.

If desired, serve hot in mugs or cups with a cinnamon stick stirrer instead of from punch bowl.

Ideal for that chilly day! Note the handy way to make this hot beverage in a percolator.

HOT SPICY CIDER

    2 cups water
    2 cups apple juice
    I cup orange juice
    ¼ teaspoon salt
    4 cinnamon sticks
    I teaspoon whole cloves
    I teaspoon whole allspice
       Orange slices

9 (½ cup) SERVINGS
46 Calories Each

In large saucepan, combine water, apple juice, orange juice and salt. Tie cinnamon sticks, cloves and allspice in a porous cloth; add to liquid. Simmer, covered, 20 minutes. Remove spice bag. Serve hot with orange slices or cinnamon stick stirrers.

Tip: For Easy Spiced Cider, add all ingredients except spices to percolator. (Cold liquids work best.) Place cinnamon sticks (break, if necessary), cloves and allspice in percolator basket. Perk as you would coffee.

CRANBERRY PUNCH

    4 cups (32 oz. or I qt.) cranberry juice
       cocktail
    1½ cups (12-oz. can) pineapple juice
    2 cups (16 oz. or ½ qt.) ginger ale, chilled*
       Ice cubes

15 (½ cup) SERVINGS
42 Calories Each

Chill all ingredients. In large mixing bowl or 2 qt. pitcher, combine cranberry juice and pineapple juice; mix well. Just before serving, stir in ginger ale and ice cubes.

Tips: *Lemon-lime carbonated beverage can be used for the ginger ale.

Recipe can be doubled for 30 (½ cup) servings.

AROUND-THE-WORLD IN A COFFEE CUP

Prepare strong hot coffee for number of persons to be served. Let guests assist in preparing their favorite around-the-world coffees from following recipes. If you are watching calories, have yours without whipped cream.

SWEDISH

40 Calories Per Cup

Spiced Base Mixture: (Enough for 24 cups coffee)
    ½ cup firmly packed brown sugar
    ½ teaspoon cinnamon
    ½ teaspoon ground cloves
    ½ teaspoon ground nutmeg

Combine ingredients; mix well.

BRAZILIAN

65 Calories Per Cup

Place 2 tablespoons instant cocoa mix in serving cup. Add strong hot coffee. Stir with cinnamon stick. Top each serving with whipped cream.

VIENNESE

39 Calories Per Cup

Pour strong hot coffee in serving cup. Stir in I teaspoon sugar. Top with whipped cream and sprinkle with nutmeg.

ITALIAN

34 Calories Per Cup

Pour strong hot coffee in serving cup. Stir in I teaspoon sugar. Sprinkle with nutmeg. Garnish with chocolate curls.

DRESS-UPS FOR PREPARED SOUPS

SOUP	ADDITIONS	GARNISHES
Chicken Noodle or Chicken Rice	Peas and carrots, chopped celery	Chopped chives
	Cubed cooked chicken, corn, cooking sherry	Shredded Cheddar cheese
	Mixed vegetables, soy sauce	Chow mein noodles
	Peas, chopped onion, curry powder	Sieved egg yolk
	Chopped green pepper, Worcestershire sauce	Caraway seed
Vegetable Beef or Beef	Tomato juice, noodles, sweet basil	Parmesan cheese
	Cubed cooked beef, chopped green pepper, carrots, mushrooms	Chopped chives
	Small meatballs, tomato pieces, burgundy	Parsley
	Tomato juice, chopped celery, chopped onion, red cooking wine	Chopped celery tops
	Cubed cooked beef, water chestnuts, mushrooms, soy sauce	Watercress
Tomato	Beef bouillon, cabbage, chopped onion, bay leaf, sherry	Crumbled bacon
	Cubed cooked beef, corn with red and green peppers	Chopped chives
	Tuna or salmon, chopped green pepper	Chopped green onions
	Lima beans, corn	Sliced wieners

Pick a can of soup, add some meat and vegetables — behold an extra hearty soup! Think of all of the tasty combinations you can enjoy by merely freeing your refrigerator of leftovers!

Not only can you use canned soup, but also dry soup mixes, frozen soup or any servings of leftover homemade soup. If you have an extra serving of rice or noodles, save it to dress-up tomato or beef soup. Whatever your tastes or notion, you can create your own variations! And there's nothing like a hot bowl of soup for lunch. It's a great way to encourage children to eat vegetables, too!

ONION SOUP, FRENCH-STYLE

6 large onions, thinly sliced
2 tablespoons butter or margarine
1½ tablespoons flour
9 bouillon cubes or 3 tablespoons instant bouillon
6 cups water
1½ teaspoons Worcestershire sauce

8 (1 cup) SERVINGS
81 Calories Each

Sauté onions in butter in saucepan until golden. Stir in flour. Add bouillon cubes, water and Worcestershire sauce. Simmer for 20 minutes, stirring occasionally.

Tip: For those not watching calories, float Parmesan Croutons on top of soup.

Delicious and so hearty, it can be your main dish. Serve with a refreshing salad and a fruity dessert.

OLD FASHIONED VEGETABLE SOUP

2½ lbs. beef shank or meaty soup bone
1 tablespoon salt
⅛ teaspoon ground thyme
6 peppercorns, if desired
1 bay leaf
2 whole allspice, if desired
2 beef bouillon cubes or 2 teaspoons instant beef bouillon
6 cups water
2 cups (2 med.) cubed peeled potato
1 cup (2 med. stalks) sliced celery
1 cup (2 med.) sliced carrots
½ cup (1 med.) chopped onion or 2 tablespoons instant minced onion
2 cups (1-lb. can) undrained tomatoes
1½ cups (12-oz. can) drained whole kernel corn

8 (1 cup) SERVINGS
101 Calories Each

In large saucepan (5 qt.), combine beef shank, salt, thyme, peppercorns, bay leaf, allspice, bouillon cubes and water. Simmer, covered, about 3 hours until meat is tender. Remove beef shank, peppercorns and bay leaf; skim off all fat. Cut meat from bone into chunks and return to soup. Add remaining ingredients. Continue simmering, covered, about 30 minutes until vegetables are tender.

Tips: Any combination of vegetables can be used in the soup. If desired, add cubed parsnips or turnips, chopped green pepper, chopped cabbage, green beans or lima beans. The calorie count will vary accordingly.

Soup can be prepared in a pressure cooker according to manufacturer's directions.

To make ahead, prepare broth, removing meat from bone. Cover and freeze up to 3 weeks, or refrigerate for about a week. Add vegetables to thawed broth and prepare as directed.

QUICK MINESTRONE SOUP

1 cup shredded cabbage
½ cup (1 stalk) sliced celery
⅓ cup (1 med.) sliced carrot
¼ cup small noodles
1 medium tomato, cut in wedges
1 medium onion, cut in wedges or 2 tablespoons minced onion
1 tablespoon parsley flakes
½ teaspoon salt
1 bay leaf
1⅔ cups water
1⅓ cups (10½-oz. can) condensed beef broth*

4 (1 cup) SERVINGS
65 Calories Each

In medium saucepan, combine all ingredients. Bring to a boil. Reduce heat; simmer, covered, for 30 to 45 minutes. Remove bay leaf; serve.

Tips: *If desired, 1⅓ cups water and 3 cubes beef bouillon or 1 tablespoon instant beef bouillon can be used for the beef broth.

To make ahead, prepare, cover and refrigerate. Reheat before serving.

CHICKEN RICE SOUP

3 lbs. stewing chicken, cut into pieces
8 cups water
1 tablespoon salt
6 peppercorns, if desired
¼ teaspoon poultry seasoning, if desired
1 cup (2 med. stalks) chopped celery
¼ cup (½ med.) chopped onion or 1 tablespoon instant minced onion
½ cup uncooked rice

8 (1 cup) SERVINGS
167 Calories Each

In large saucepan (5 qt.), combine chicken, water, salt, peppercorns and poultry seasoning. Bring to a boil. Cover; simmer 2 to 2½ hours until chicken is tender. Remove chicken and peppercorns. Skim off all fat. Cut meat from bone into chunks and return to soup. Add remaining ingredients. Continue simmering, covered, about 30 minutes until rice is tender.

Tips: Soup can be prepared in a pressure cooker according to manufacturer's directions.

To make ahead, prepare broth, removing meat from bone. Cover and freeze up to 3 weeks or refrigerate for about a week. Add remaining ingredients to thawed broth and prepare as directed.

Main Dishes

Delicious roasted on a rotisserie, over an open fire or in the oven. Time this delicious roast carefully so it will be at desired doneness when ready to serve. For rotisserie, follow manufacturers' instructions, allowing for size of fire and distance from heat when barbecuing.

ROLLED RIB ROAST

Rolled rib roast or rib eye roast
Salt
Pepper

OVEN 325° ALLOW ½ to ¾ LB. PER SERVING
302 Calories Per Slice
(4 x 2½ x ½-inch)

Season roast with salt and pepper. Place roast, fat side up, on rack in open shallow roasting pan. Insert meat thermometer so bulb reaches center of thickest part. (Do not add water; do not cover.) Roast at 325° to desired degree of doneness. For ease in carving, let stand 15 minutes. To serve, cut across grain into slices.

Timetable for Roasting

	Doneness	Approx. Cooking Time per Lb.	Meat Thermometer Reading
Rolled Rib Roast	Rare	32 min.	140°
	Medium	38 min.	160°
	Well	48 min.	170°
Rib Eye Roast	Rare	18 to 20 min.	140°
	Medium	20 to 22 min.	160°
	Well	22 to 24 min.	170°

Tips: Boneless rolled rump and sirloin tip roasts of high quality can be roasted as above. Roast at 325° until medium to well done, allowing 25 to 30 minutes per pound for rump roast and 35 to 40 minutes per pound for sirloin tip.

To prepare on rotisserie, follow instructions with oven or grill rotisserie using a meat thermometer to assure desired degree of doneness. Time will vary from 2 to 5 hours depending on size and shape of cut, temperature when cooking begins, and the heat maintained during cooking.

Standing rib roast is especially nice for carving and serving at the table. Plan your timing so it will be just at the right degree of doneness when ready to serve.

STANDING BEEF RIB ROAST

Standing rib roast
Salt
Pepper

OVEN 325° ALLOW ½ TO ¾ LB. PER SERVING
302 Calories Per Slice
(4 x 2½ x ½-inch)

Season roast with salt and pepper. Place roast, fat side up, on rack in open shallow roasting pan. Insert meat thermometer so the bulb reaches the center of the largest muscle, being sure that the bulb does not rest in fat or on bone. (Do not add water; do not cover.) Roast at 325° to desired degree of doneness.

Timetable For Roasting

Weight	Doneness	Meat Thermometer Reading	Approx. Cooking Time per lb.
4 to 6 lbs.	rare	140°	26 to 32 min.
	medium	160°	34 to 38 min.
	well	170°	40 to 42 min.
6 to 8 lbs.	rare	140°	23 to 25 min.
	medium	160°	27 to 30 min.
	well	170°	32 to 35 min.

How To Carve

Place the roast on the platter with the largest end down to form a solid base. Insert the fork between the two top ribs. Starting on the fat side, carve across the grain to the rib bone.

Use the tip of the knife to cut along the rib bone to loosen the slice. Be sure to keep close to the bone, to make the largest number of servings possible.

Slide the knife back under the slice and, steadying it with the fork, lift the slice to the side of the platter. If the platter is not large enough, place the slices on a heated platter close by.

ROASTS (cooked without liquid)

Standing Rib Roast: A roast cut from the tender rib area; contains the rib bones. In restaurants it's served as "Prime Rib".

Rolled Rib Roast: A rib roast with bone removed, rolled and tied.

Rib Eye Roast: The large muscle from the rib roast. Also referred to as Delmonico Roast.

Tenderloin: Tenderest muscle in beef; the small tender muscle you see on a T-bone or Porterhouse Steak. When left whole it makes a long, tapering tender roast. When cut into 1 to 2-inch thick pieces it is called Tenderloin Steak or Filet Mignon.

Rolled Rump: A boneless, rolled roast from rump area; a less tender roast than rib, however very good roasted if of high quality meat.

Sirloin Tip: A roast from the round steak area with a small tip of the sirloin included. Can be roasted if of high quality meat.

Seasonings, Spices and Herbs for Beef:

Tabasco sauce, tomato sauce, barbecue sauce, garlic, herb or wine vinegar, curry, ginger, mustard, paprika, pepper, allspice, celery seed, chili powder, ground cloves, rosemary, savory, tarragon, thyme, basil, bay leaf, marjoram, oregano.

POT-ROASTS

Blade Bone Roast: From the shoulder (chuck area); contains the blade bone and sometimes backbone. Usually less expensive than arm bone, but there is more bone and waste. Sometimes referred to as Chuck Roast.

Arm Bone Roast: From the shoulder (chuck area); contains the round arm bone. (Can tell from round steak bone by bone being nearer center of cut and by several small meat muscles surrounding it.) Sometimes called Chuck Roast.

Rump Roast: From the rump area of animal. Usually a more expensive cut than Blade Cut or Arm Chuck Roasts, but there is less waste from bone and fat.

Heel of Round: Cut from the end of the round steak area where there is no bone. A little less tender than rump roast.

OVEN BAKED POT-ROAST

    3 lbs. arm, chuck or blade pot-roast
    ½ cup (I envelope) dry onion soup mix
    3 to 4 medium potatoes, cut into quarters
    4 carrots, cut into quarters
    I large stalk celery, cut into pieces

OVEN 350°   8 SERVINGS
                       498 Calories Each*

Place pot-roast in baking dish or casserole with cover. Sprinkle onion soup mix over meat. Cover; bake at 350° for 2 to 2½ hours. Add potatoes, carrots and celery; cover and continue baking for I hour.

Tip: *Chuck pot-roast contains more fat between the muscle tissues so the calories will be higher. Arm or blade pot-roast will have 354 Calories Per Serving.

Marinate the meat 24 hours for a milder flavored sauerbraten; 48 hours if you like a stronger flavor. For those not watching calories, gingersnaps make a quick and flavorful thickening for a tasty sauce.

SAUERBRATEN

    3 lbs. heel of round, rump or sirloin
       tip roast
    I cup red wine vinegar
    1½ cups water
    ½ cup (I med.) sliced onion
    ½ cup (I stalk) sliced celery
    5 whole cloves
    2 bay leaves
    I tablespoon (3 tsp.) salt
    4 peppercorns or ¼ teaspoon pepper
    I tablespoon oil or shortening

                             8 SERVINGS
                       399 Calories Each

Place meat in deep bowl. Add remaining ingredients except oil. Cover and marinate in refrigerator 24 to 48 hours, turning meat several times to season evenly. Remove meat from marinade; drain well. In Dutch oven, brown meat in hot oil on all sides. Add 1½ cups of strained marinade. Cover and simmer 2½ to 3 hours until tender.

Tip: For flavorful gingersnap sauce, spoon fat off of juices. Add 2 tablespoons brown sugar and 6 crushed gingersnaps to juices. Cook, stirring constantly until mixture comes to a boil. If necessary, thin with water or remaining marinade. Pour over meat. Remove meat to heated platter.

Pot-roast is economical and delicious. Start 3 hours ahead and allow to simmer; or see Tip for making ahead. Serve with a crispy salad.

BEEF POT-ROAST WITH VEGETABLES

   3 lbs. arm, blade, chuck, or rump pot-roast
   I tablespoon oil or shortening
2½ cups water
   2 teaspoons salt
   ¼ teaspoon pepper
   I bay leaf
   4 medium onions, sliced
   3 stalks celery, cut into pieces
   4 medium carrots, cut into pieces
   4 medium potatoes, peeled and cut in half

8 SERVINGS
463 Calories Each

Brown pot-roast on both sides in oil in heavy fry pan or Dutch oven for about 15 minutes. Add water, salt, pepper, bay leaf, I onion and I stalk celery. Cover tightly and simmer 2 to 2½ hours until meat is tender. Add remaining vegetables; simmer 45 to 60 minutes until tender. Remove meat and vegetables to heated platter. Serve with juices.

Tips: Part red wine (about I cup) can be used for part of water.

Use other vegetables too: rutabagas, mushrooms or cabbage wedges.

For Easy Pot-Roast, omit salt, pepper and first addition of onion and celery; add I envelope dry onion soup mix with water.

To make ahead, prepare except for adding vegetables; cook, refrigerate or freeze. To serve, add vegetables and simmer 45 minutes.

Just place this foil-wrapped pot-roast in the oven 3 hours ahead, then forget about it until time to serve. Make an oven meal by baking potatoes and a vegetable during the last hour.

POT-ROAST IN FOIL

   3 lbs. chuck, arm or blade pot-roast
   ½ cup (I envelope) dry onion soup mix

OVEN 350°   8 SERVINGS
305 Calories Each

Trim excess fat from meat. Place meat in center of a piece of heavy duty foil; sprinkle with dry soup mix. Bring edges of foil together and seal with double fold; seal ends with double fold.

Place seam-side up in shallow baking pan. Bake at 350° for 2½ to 3 hours until meat is tender.

Tip: For variety, add one of the following along with soup: sliced fresh or canned mushrooms, sliced celery, sliced carrots or green pepper rings.

For a different twist to pot-roast, try this recipe with a barbecue sauce. Plan it around your schedule — start 2¼ hours ahead, or prepare partially the night before and then reheat. Serve with hot asparagus and a crispy salad.

OVEN BARBECUED POT-ROAST

   3 lbs. arm, blade or chuck pot-roast

Barbecue Sauce

   I cup (8-oz. can) tomato sauce
   ¼ cup red wine or water
   2 tablespoons brown sugar
   ½ teaspoon salt
   2 teaspoons prepared or I teaspoon dry
      mustard
   I clove garlic, minced, or ⅛ teaspoon
      instant minced garlic or garlic powder
   I medium onion, sliced
   ½ lemon, sliced

OVEN 350°   8 SERVINGS
465 Calories Each*

In large saucepan, cover roast with water; salt to taste. Simmer, covered, over medium low heat 1½ hours (meanwhile prepare Barbecue Sauce). Drain; place roast in baking dish. Pour Barbecue Sauce over roast, coating roast well. Cover tightly with lid or foil. Bake at 350° for 45 to 60 minutes until tender.

Barbecue Sauce: Combine all ingredients.

Tips: *Chuck pot-roast contains more fat between the muscle tissues, so the calories will be higher. Arm or blade pot-roast will have 320 Calories Per Serving.

To reheat, add a little water; cover and reheat at 325° for about 30 minutes.

To make ahead, pour Barbecue Sauce over partially cooked meat in baking dish; cool, cover and refrigerate. Bake at 350° for about I hour until meat is tender and heated through.

This dish freezes well. Add a little water before reheating.

PEPPER STEAK

1½ lbs. flank steak
2 tablespoons flour
1 tablespoon shortening
1 beef bouillon cube or 1 teaspoon instant beef bouillon
½ teaspoon salt
⅛ teaspoon garlic powder or ½ teaspoon garlic salt
⅛ teaspoon pepper
1 cup water
2 green peppers, cut into 2-inch squares

6 SERVINGS
196 Calories Each

Cut flank steak into ¼-inch strips. Coat with flour. Heat oil in large fry pan; brown meat over medium high heat. Add bouillon, salt, garlic powder, pepper and water. Simmer, covered, 1½ hours. Add green pepper; continue simmering ½ hour.

MUSHROOM TOPPED FLANK STEAK

1½ lbs. flank steak or round steak, cut ½-inch thick
1 teaspoon butter or margarine
½ cup (1 med.) chopped onion
1 cup (8 oz.) sliced fresh mushrooms or ½ cup (4-oz.) sliced canned mushrooms
2 tablespoons chopped parsley or 1 tablespoon parsley flakes
½ teaspoon salt
¼ teaspoon pepper
¼ teaspoon poultry seasoning or ground thyme, if desired
1 cup water or ⅓ cup red wine and ⅔ cup water

6 SERVINGS
186 Calories Each

Cut steak into 6 pieces or leave whole. Brown in butter in hot fry pan. After browned on one side, turn; top with onions and mushrooms. Sprinkle with parsley, salt, pepper and poultry seasoning. Pour water over all. Lower heat; cover and simmer for 1½ to 2 hours until tender. If desired, garnish with additional parsley before serving.

Tip: Steak can be prepared in an electric fry pan. Brown at 400°; simmer at 250° as directed.

STEAKS (tender)

T-Bone Steak: Bone has distinct T shape; on one side of bone is small tenderloin muscle, on other side is large loin muscle.

Rib Steak: Cut from the rib area — similar to rib roast only cut into 1 to 2-inch thick steaks.

Club Steak: Similar to rib steak but it may be seen with a small portion of tenderloin.

Porterhouse Steak: Similar to a T-bone but larger in size. Tenderloin is larger in this cut than in other steaks.

Sirloin Steak: A large tender steak that contains several large muscles; may be boneless or contain small wedge or flat bone.

STEAKS (less tender)

Round Steak: Characteristic round bone with 1 large muscle above bone (often separated and sold as top round) and 2 smaller muscles below bone (often separated and sold as bottom round). The small muscle is sometimes separated and sold as eye of round steak.

Chuck Steak: Chuck is another term for shoulder and associated with pot-roasts. Chuck Steak is from this area and cut 1 to 2 inches thick. It usually contains the blade bone (like in a Blade Pot-Roast) or arm bone (like in an Arm Pot-Roast). Sometimes called barbecue steak but needs tenderizing before grilling.

Flank Steak: Sometimes called London Broil or Plank Steak. This boneless steak comes from the less tender flank area. It can be very flavorful if tenderized, broiled rare and carved across the long muscle into thin slices when served; or simmer with liquid.

Family Steak: Usually cut from the round of sirloin area. They are often recommended for barbecuing, although we suggest some type of marinating or tenderizing before barbecuing or broiling, especially if from round steak area.

CUBE STEAK

Less tender pieces of meat that are made tender by mechanical cubing or cutting through fibers. Also sold as Minute Steak.

An easy to prepare company meal when you prepare the meat, vegetables and soy sauce mixture early; then cover and refrigerate. Just start cooking 15 minutes before serving time.

4 SERVINGS
317 Calories Each

SUKIYAKI

  1 lb. sirloin tip or sirloin steak
  1 tablespoon oil or shortening
  ½ cup soy sauce
  ⅔ cup water
  2 tablespoons sugar
  ½ teaspoon MSG (monosodium glutamate),
    if desired
  ¾ cup (5-oz. can) drained bamboo shoots
  1 cup green onions, cut into 1-inch pieces
  2 medium onions, thinly sliced
  2 cups (1-lb. can) drained bean sprouts
  ⅔ cup (5-oz. can) sliced water chestnuts
  1 cup sliced fresh or canned mushrooms

Cut meat into paper-thin slices across the grain, (freezing meat makes slicing easier), then into strips 1-inch wide. Brown strips in hot oil in large fry pan 2 to 3 minutes. Combine soy sauce, water, sugar and MSG. Pour over meat. Push meat to one side of fry pan. Keeping the ingredients separate, add bamboo shoots, green onions and onion slices. Cook 5 to 10 minutes, turning vegetables and keeping separate. Push vegetables to one side. Add bean sprouts, water chestnuts and mushrooms, keeping ingredients separate. Cook 2 minutes until hot. Serve with rice.

Tip: An electric fry pan set at 400° to 425° can be used to cook Sukiyaki.

71

Perfect fare for a cold, winter day. Start cooking 4 hours ahead.

NEW ENGLAND BOILED DINNER

3 lbs. corned beef
I bay leaf
I teaspoon peppercorns, if desired
6 potatoes, peeled and quartered
6 carrots, cut in half lengthwise
6 wedges (I med. head) cabbage

8 SERVINGS
604 Calories Each

In large saucepan, cover corned beef with water. Add bay leaf and peppercorns. Cover and simmer over low heat 3 to 3½ hours until tender. Add potatoes and carrots. Cover and simmer 15 minutes. Add cabbage; cook 15 minutes longer until vegetables are tender. Cut meat into pieces. Serve with broth and vegetables.

Tips: To make ahead, cook corned beef; remove bay leaf and refrigerate or freeze. Reheat and add vegetables, continuing as directed.

Serve leftover corned beef in sandwiches.

TANGY BEEF BROIL

I to 2 tablespoons vinegar
I tablespoon Worcestershire sauce
I tablespoon Dijon or prepared mustard or
I teaspoon dry mustard
8 slices (¾ lb.) cooked beef

BROIL | 4 SERVINGS
155 Calories Each

Combine vinegar, Worcestershire sauce and mustard; mix well. Place beef slices on ungreased broiler pan or cookie sheet. Brush with mustard mixture. Broil 4 to 5 inches from heat for 2 minutes on first side. Turn; brush other side with mustard mixture. Continue broiling 2 minutes until heated through.

Tip: Steak, trimmed of all fat, can be used for the cooked beef. Broil as directed on page 68, basting occasionally with mustard mixture.

Flank steak becomes tender and flavorful as it marinates in teriyaki marinade. Serve with rice, green beans and a fruit dessert.

TERIYAKI STEAK

½ cup (5-oz. bottle) soy sauce
I clove garlic, minced or ⅛ teaspoon instant minced garlic
2 tablespoons brown sugar
½ teaspoon powdered ginger
2 tablespoons Worcestershire sauce
I tablespoon lemon juice
1½ lbs. flank steak

6 SERVINGS
198 Calories Each

In shallow bowl or plastic bag, combine all ingredients except flank steak. Add steak, coating with marinade. Cover tightly and refrigerate 6 to 24 hours, turning occasionally. Remove from marinade. Broil or grill over hot coals, placing about 2 inches from heat and broiling about 5 minutes on each side. To serve, cut across the grain into thin slices.

Tip: Prepared teriyaki sauce can be used for the soy sauce, garlic, brown sugar, ginger, Worcestershire sauce and lemon juice.

Flank Steak makes an economical, flavorful steak, but should be medium rare to assure tenderness. Delicious served plain. Ready to eat in 15 minutes.

LONDON BROIL

2 lbs. flank steak
Meat tenderizer, if desired
2 tablespoons butter or margarine, melted
Pepper

8 SERVINGS
257 Calories Each

Score flank steak on each side at I-inch intervals. Prepare steak with meat tenderizer as directed on label. Place steak on rack in broiling pan and broil 3 inches from heat for 5 minutes. Brush with butter and season with pepper. Turn and broil 5 minutes longer until medium rare. Cut on the diagonal, across grain, into very thin slices.

Tip: For garlic flavor, add clove of garlic to butter when melting.

Meat Buying and Storing Tips

Meat selection is often one of the most difficult tasks. The variety of names used for a particular cut plus the continuing change going on with meat names can be very discouraging. By learning a few basics about the distinctive appearance of particular meat cuts, you need not be confused when it appears with a new name. If you aren't sure about a cut, ask where it comes from in relation to cuts you are familiar with — it makes a big difference if it comes from the T-bone steak area or if it comes from the pot-roast area. You must know what you're buying in order to cook it so that it will be tender and flavorful.

Some thoughts to keep in mind when selecting meat:

1. Meat becomes less tender with exercise. For example, a beef chuck (shoulder) where pot-roasts come from has much more exercise than the back where tender steaks come from.

2. Meat becomes less tender with age. For example, most cuts of veal and lamb (young animals) are tender, but only certain portions of beef are tender.

3. Although exercise makes meat less tender, it does develop flavor. For example, some people prefer the delicate flavor of tenderloin steak (receives almost no exercise) whereas some prefer the heartier flavor of a sirloin steak (receives moderate exercise). Or, a tender steak would make poor stew meat because the juices would have little flavor.

4. The shoulder (chuck) and round area are often confused since both may have a round bone (arm in shoulder, leg in round). In all meats — beef, veal, pork and lamb — the shoulder consists of many muscles running in various directions, plus many cuts also have a portion of the blade bone. Meats from this area usually cost less per pound because there are more cuts from this section than from the tenderloin section. Sometimes there's also more waste. Meats from the round area have about 3 large solid muscles all running in the same direction. Since there is less exercise here, the cuts tend to be slightly more tender.

5. Any cut of meat can be made tender with proper cooking. Tender, delicate flavored cuts (like T-bone steak) are best cooked quickly without added water; whereas a less tender cut is best cooked with liquid. The long cooking with liquid tenderizes the less tender meat tissues. Some tenderizing of less tender meats can result from marinating in a marinade for several hours or overnight. Most marinades contain lemon juice, vinegar or wine — the acid in these helps soften and tenderize the less tender tissues.

Guide for Amount of Meat to Purchase:

Use this as a general guide considering your family's eating habits and the other foods that will be served with the meal.

Meat with no bone and very little fat — ¼ to ⅓ lb. per serving.

Meat with small amount of bone and little fat — ⅓ to ½ lb. per serving.

Meat with large amount of bone and little fat — ¾ to 1 lb. per serving.

When looking for good meat buys, consider the price per lb. in relation to the amount you will need to purchase for a serving.

Storage of Meat:

1. Store in the coldest part of refrigerator without actually freezing the meat. A refrigerator meat storage compartment is specially designed for optimum temperature and humidity.

2. Pre-packaged meats can be stored in their original wrappings for 1 to 2 days. For longer storage (up to 3 days) unwrap meat and cover loosely — some air helps retard bacteria growth. Large cuts of meat (roasts) can be stored 5 to 6 days. Ground meats should be used within 24 hours. If you find you cannot use the meat right away, freeze or cook and freeze; then thaw and cook or reheat to serve.

3. You can freeze meat in original packaging for short storage, 1 to 2 weeks. For longer storage, overwrap or rewrap in moisture-vapor proof material and store in freezer (not refrigerator-freezer) at 0° or lower. Beef can be stored 6 to 12 months; veal and lamb 6 to 9 months; pork 3 to 6 months; smoked ham and fresh pork sausage 2 months; corned beef 2 weeks. Freezing is not recommended for canned hams and other canned meats, as freezing sometimes causes seams in the can to break.

How to Judge When Meat is Spoiled:

Meat that is spoiling changes from a bright red for beef and lamb (or pink for pork and veal) to a dull greyed color. The surface may become slippery and the meat develops a pronounced off-odor. When an off-odor has developed the meat should be discarded.

A quick and easy stroganoff made with ground beef and mushrooms. Serve over rice or noodles, along with carrots and a salad in just 30 minutes.

STROGANOFF WITH GROUND BEEF

I lb. lean ground beef
½ cup (I small) chopped onion
⅔ cup (4-oz. can) drained mushroom stems and pieces
¼ cup water, red wine or beef broth
I teaspoon Worcestershire sauce
½ teaspoon salt
¼ teaspoon celery seed
Dash pepper
½ cup plain yogurt

4 SERVINGS
236 Calories Each

In fry pan, brown ground beef and onion. Drain well; blot excess fat with paper towel. Stir in mushrooms, water, Worcestershire sauce, salt, celery seed and pepper. Cover and simmer for I5 to 20 minutes. Stir in yogurt; heat through, but do not boil. If desired, garnish with parsley.

Tip: For an oven casserole, combine cooked mixture and 2 cups cooked noodles in a I½ to 2-quart casserole. Bake, covered, at 350° for 20 minutes until heated through.

A budget minded and easy-to-prepare variation on chow mein. Serve with a green vegetable and a fruity dessert.

CHOP-CHOP CHOW MEIN

I lb. lean ground beef
¼ cup (½ med.) chopped onion or
I tablespoon instant minced onion
I½ cups (3 stalks) sliced celery
¼ cup flour
I teaspoon salt
2 cups (I-lb. can) tomato juice
½ cup (4-oz. can) undrained mushrooms
2 cups (I-lb. can) drained bean sprouts
Soy sauce

6 SERVINGS
184 Calories Each

In large fry pan, fry ground beef. Drain thoroughly, using paper towel to absorb all excess fat. Add onion and celery; continue cooking until onions are tender. Stir in flour and salt. Add tomato juice, mushrooms and bean sprouts. Continue cooking until heated through. Simmer, uncovered, for I5 to 20 minutes. Serve hot with soy sauce over rice.

Tip: For those not watching calories, salted almonds can be used as a garnish.

Meatballs take on an Hawaiian flavor with this sweet-sour pineapple and green pepper sauce. Serve in about 40 minutes with Chinese pea pods and a salad of cottage cheese on lettuce.

SWEET 'N SOUR MEATBALLS

I lb. lean ground beef
¼ cup dry bread or cracker crumbs
2 tablespoons finely chopped onion or
½ teaspoon instant minced onion
½ teaspoon salt
⅛ teaspoon pepper
I½ cups (I-lb. 4-oz. can) water-packed pineapple tidbits or chunks, drain and reserve ½ cup liquid
2 tablespoons sugar
I tablespoon cornstarch
2 tablespoons soy sauce
2 tablespoons vinegar
½ cup water
Reserved ½ cup pineapple liquid
I½ to 2 green peppers, cut into I-inch pieces

4 SERVINGS
310 Calories Each

In large mixing bowl, combine ground beef, bread crumbs, onion, salt and pepper; mix well. Shape into I-inch balls. Place in cold fry pan. Turn heat on gradually; (fat in meatballs will melt and prevent sticking). Brown meatballs well. Drain off drippings; remove meatballs. Drain pineapple, reserving ½ cup liquid. Combine sugar and cornstarch in fry pan, stir in soy sauce, vinegar, water and pineapple liquid. Cook, stirring constantly, until mixture boils and thickens. Add green pepper, pineapple and meatballs. Cover and simmer I5 to 20 minutes. Serve over rice.

Tip: To make ahead, prepare, cool and refrigerate or freeze. To serve, reheat, adding additional water if necessary.

*Delight your family with this hearty dish —
so hearty you'll only need to add a salad and
a fruity dessert to complete your meal. Start
fixing it about 1½ hours before supper.*

STUFFED PEPPERS

    6 large green peppers
      Boiling water
 1½ lbs. lean ground beef
  ¼ cup (½ med.) finely chopped onion or
      1 tablespoon instant minced onion
  ½ cup (1 stalk) chopped celery
  ½ cup chopped green pepper, if desired
  ½ teaspoon salt
    2 cups cooked rice

Creole Sauce

    2 cups (1-lb. can) undrained tomatoes
  ¼ cup chopped onion or 1 tablespoon
      instant minced onion
  ½ teaspoon salt
    1 tablespoon sugar
    1 teaspoon leaf basil
    1 tablespoon flour
  ¼ cup water

OVEN 350°   6 SERVINGS
                              315 Calories Each

Cut tops from peppers; remove membranes
and seeds. In large saucepan, cover peppers
with boiling water. Cook, uncovered, 10 minutes; drain. Brown ground beef; drain
thoroughly, using paper towel to absorb excess
fat. Add onion, celery and green pepper to
ground beef; continue cooking to brown
lightly. Add salt and rice; mix well. Spoon
mixture into peppers. Place peppers in baking
dish or 2½ to 3-quart casserole and top with
Creole Sauce. Bake, covered, at 350° for
45 minutes; uncover and continue baking for
15 minutes.

Creole Sauce:

Combine tomatoes, onion, salt, sugar and
basil in fry pan. Simmer 10 minutes. Combine
flour and water; add to fry pan and cook until
mixture thickens.

*What a great variation to ground beef.
Draining the cooked beef of all excess fat
further reduces calories. Serve with a green
vegetable and coleslaw for a yummy supper.*

BEEF STUFFED CABBAGE LEAVES

    8 large cabbage leaves
  ½ lb. lean ground beef
    1 egg
  ½ cup (1 med.) chopped onion or
      2 tablespoons instant minced onion
    1 cup cooked rice
    1 teaspoon salt
  ¼ teaspoon pepper
    1 cup (8-oz. can) undrained cooked
      tomatoes
  ½ teaspoon leaf thyme or ⅛ teaspoon
      ground thyme
    2 tablespoons minced parsley or 1 teaspoon
      parsley flakes

                                   4 SERVINGS
                              315 Calories Each

In large saucepan, cook cabbage leaves in
salted water for 5 minutes. Drain. Brown
ground beef in large fry pan. Drain thoroughly,
using paper towel to absorb all excess fat. Add
egg, ¼ cup of the onion, rice, salt and pepper;
continue browning until onions are tender.
Place 1 spoonful meat mixture on each leaf.
Fold edges in and roll up. Fasten each with
wooden pick. Combine tomatoes, remaining
¼ cup of the onion, thyme and parsley in fry
pan. Place cabbage rolls in tomato mixture.
Simmer, covered, for 45 minutes.

Tip: To make ahead, roll meat mixture in
cabbage leaves and top with tomato mixture
as directed. Cover and refrigerate. Before
serving, simmer, covered, for 45 minutes.

GROUND BEEF

Meat and trimming from less tender sections
that are ground by mechanical means. Lean
ground beef contains less fat than ground beef;
ground chuck is from the chuck (shoulder)
area; ground round is from the round steak
area and ground sirloin is from the sirloin steak
area.

HAMBURGER PIE

 I lb. lean ground beef
 ¼ cup chopped onion or I tablespoon
      instant minced onion
 I teaspoon salt
 ¼ teaspoon pepper
 I tablespoon Worcestershire sauce
 2 cups (I recipe) Easy Mashed Potatoes,
      page 108
 I egg
      Dash garlic salt, if desired
 2 cups (16-oz. can) drained, cut green beans
      Dash paprika

OVEN 350°   4 SERVINGS
                                321 Calories Each

Combine ground beef, onion, salt, pepper
and Worcestershire sauce; mix well. Press
mixture over bottom and sides of ungreased
9-inch pie pan to form a crust. Bake at 350°
for 20 minutes. Meanwhile, prepare potatoes;
beat in egg and garlic salt. Drain fat from meat
shell using paper towel to absorb excess fat.
Spoon beans unto meat shell; top with mashed
potatoes. Sprinkle with paprika. Continue
baking for 20 to 30 minutes until potatoes are
lightly browned. Cut into wedges; serve.

MEATLOAF

 I lb. lean ground beef
 2 tablespoon chopped onion or 2 teaspoons
      instant minced onion
 ½ to I teaspoon salt
 ¼ teaspoon pepper
 ¼ teaspoon chili powder
 2 tablespoons skim milk
 I tablespoon Worcestershire sauce
 I egg
 2 tablespoons catsup

OVEN 350°   4 SERVINGS
                                239 Calories Each

In medium mixing bowl, combine all ingredients; mix well. Form meat mixture in loaf
shape on broiler rack in broiler pan. (As meat
cooks, fat will drip off and reduce calories.)
Top with catsup. Bake at 350° for 45 to
50 minutes.

Tips: For Burgundy Beef Patties, place patties
made from ¼ cup meat mixture into cold fry
pan. Turn on heat; brown slowly. Drain fat.
Add ¼ cup Burgundy or other red wine and
¼ cup water. Simmer, covered, 15 minutes.

Serve with juices.

For Baked Meatballs, shape I tablespoon meat
mixture into a ball by rolling gently between
palms. Place on broiler rack in broiler pan.
(As meat cooks, fat will drip off and reduce
calories.) Bake at 350° for 20 to 25 minutes
until brown and somewhat firm.

For Broiled Meatballs, place meatballs on
broiler rack of broiler pan. Broil 4 to 5 inches
from heat for 7 to 10 minutes until done.

HAMBURGERS

 I lb. lean ground beef
 I teaspoon salt
 ⅛ teaspoon pepper
 I tablespoon Worcestershire sauce
      Dash Tabasco sauce

                                   4 SERVINGS
                                206 Calories Each

Combine ground beef with Worcestershire
sauce and Tabasco sauce. Shape into patties.
In fry pan, fry patties over medium heat 5 to
10 minutes on each side, until browned to
desired doneness. If desired, serve with onion
slices, mustard and catsup.

Tips: Patties are also good broiled or barbe-
cued over hot coals. Broil 15 minutes for rare
and 25 minutes for medium.

The following seasonings can be used for the
Worcestershire sauce and Tabasco sauce:
2 to 4 tablespoons chopped onion, I tablespoon instant minced onion or I tablespoon
onion salt.
½ teaspoon garlic salt, ⅛ teaspoon garlic
powder or ⅛ teaspoon instant minced garlic.
I tablespoon Barbecue Sauce.
I teaspoon prepared mustard and/or
I tablespoon catsup.

For Cheeseburgers, top each hamburger with
I slice cheese during last minute of frying.
Cover until cheese begins to melt.

Filled hamburgers: Form each patty into two
thin patties. Place desired filling between
patties; seal edges well.

Filling Suggestions:
Slices of cheese
Chopped canned mushrooms
Mustard
Catsup
Pickle relish
Chopped or sliced pickle

SLIM JIM CHILI

I lb. lean ground beef
½ cup (I med.) chopped onion
2 cups (3 to 4 stalks) sliced celery, if desired
½ cup chopped green pepper
½ teaspoon garlic salt
1¾ cups (15-oz. can) undrained kidney beans
4 cups (two I-lb. cans) undrained tomatoes
1½ to 2½ teaspoons salt
½ to I tablespoon chili powder
I bay leaf

8 (I cup) SERVINGS
156 Calories Each

Brown meat and onion in Dutch oven or large fry pan; thoroughly drain all excess fat. Add remaining ingredients. Simmer, covered, I to 2 hours. Remove bay leaf; serve hot.

Tip: This dish freezes well.

Why not give hamburgers a new flavor treat next time you serve them? Marinate in a spicy or tomato sauce, broil or grill. You'll enjoy them! Make ahead.

BARBECUED HAMBURGERS

Spicy Barbecue Sauce, page 97*

I lb. lean ground beef
I teaspoon salt

BROIL

4 HAMBURGERS
210 Calories Each

Prepare Spicy Barbecue Sauce, page 97. Set aside. Combine ground beef with salt. Shape into 4 patties. Place patties in shallow baking pan; pour sauce over patties and marinate several hours at room temperature or overnight in refrigerator. Remove hamburger patties from marinade and place on broiler pan. Broil 4 to 6 inches from heat 5 to 8 minutes. Turn; brush with marinade. Broil 5 to 8 minutes until of desired doneness.

Tips: *Tomato Barbecue Sauce, page 96, can be used for the Spicy Barbecue Sauce.

To grill over hot coals, prepare hamburgers as directed. Grill 6 inches above hot coals for 5 to 8 minutes on each side, brushing each hamburger with I teaspoon sauce after turning.

Poultry may be government inspected and graded; however, it is not required and the grade is seldom indicated in the retail market.

"Ready-to-cook" poultry is eviscerated and the head and feet removed. Most poultry sold is in this form. It may be purchased whole, split in half, quartered or cut-up pieces.

"Dressed" poultry has the feathers removed but is weighed with viscera, head and feet.

Frozen poultry is generally available whole or in pieces. Since it is frozen very shortly after processing, it is sometimes fresher than unfrozen poultry. Frozen turkey is also available — stuffed or processed as a boneless roll.

Chickens are classified by age into "broilers," "fryers," "roasting chickens," "stewing chickens" or fowl. Younger chickens are lighter in weight, have less fat, are more tender and require less cooking. Older chickens are less expensive and require longer, moist heat cooking.

Capons are larger than hens and are usually selected for roasting rather than frying.

Seasonings, Spices and Herbs for Poultry:

Tabasco sauce, horseradish, lemon juice, soy sauce, tomato sauce, barbecue sauce, chili sauce, garlic, herb or wine vinegar, curry powder, ginger, mustard, nutmeg, paprika, pepper, saffron, celery seed, chili powder, parsley, rosemary, sage, savory, tarragon, bay leaf, marjoram, oregano.

For cubed cooked chicken, you can use leftover chicken, canned chicken or a cooked, fresh stewing chicken. One 3-lb. 4-oz. can whole chicken yields about 2½ cups cubed chicken. A 5-lb. stewing chicken yields 5 cups cubed cooked chicken plus about 4 cups broth. Prepare as directed below:

STEWED CHICKEN

4 to 5 lbs. stewing chicken, cut-up
4 cups water
I medium onion, sliced
I medium stalk celery, chopped
2 or 3 peppercorns, if desired

382 Calories Per I Cup Chicken
23 Calories Per ½ Cup Broth

In large saucepan, combine all ingredients. Cover and simmer 2 to 3 hours until tender. Remove chicken; strain broth. Cool chicken slightly; skim off all fat. Remove skin and bones; cut into pieces. Cover and refrigerate. Use within two days or wrap tightly and freeze.

Tips: Chicken may be cooked in pressure cooker according to manufacturer's directions.

Turkey can be substituted for chicken, too. A 3-lbs. turkey roast yields about 5 cups cubed cooked turkey.

Timetable for Roasting Stuffed Chilled Poultry

Kind of Poultry		Ready-to-Cook Weight Pounds	Approx. Amount of Stuffing Quarts	Approx. Total Roasting Time Hours	
CHICKEN				325°F.	400°F.
	Broilers or Fryers	1½ to 2½	¼ to ½	1¼ to 2	I to 2*
	Roasters	2½ to 4½	½ to 1¼	2 to 3½	1¾ to 3#
	Capons	4 to 8	1¼ to 1¾	3 to 5	
TURKEY					
	Fryers or roasters (very young birds)	4 to 8	I to 2	3 to 4½	
	Roasters (fully grown young birds)	6 to 12	1½ to 3	3½ to 5	
		12 to 14	3 to 4	5 to 5¾	
		14 to 18	4 to 5	5¾ to 6	
		18 to 24	5 to 6	6 to 6¾	
	Halves, quarters, half breasts	3½ to 5	I to 1½	3 to 3½	
		5 to 8	1½ to 2	3½ to 4	
		8 to 12	2 to 3	4 to 5	

* Or roast unstuffed ¾ to 1½ hours.
# Or roast unstuffed 1½ to 2¾ hours.

Roast Chicken or Turkey

Remove giblets from body cavity. If necessary, remove pinfeathers. Rinse inside and out with cold water; dry. Remove any bits of lung, kidney or windpipe. Rub salt (⅛ teaspoon per pound of bird) on inside of neck and body cavities. Place stuffing in neck and body cavities **just before roasting.** Allow 1 cup stuffing per pound of ready-to-cook weight or ¾ cup stuffing per pound of dressed weight. Do not pack tightly as stuffing must have space to expand during cooking. Fold neck skin to back; skewer. Close body cavity with skewers and lace with string. Fold wings to back of bird by lifting a wing up and out and forcing the tip back until it rests flat against the back. Tie drumsticks to tail. Place on a rack in a shallow open pan with the breast up. If V-shaped rack is used, roast bird breast side down. Brush skin of bird thoroughly with melted fat or butter. If a roast meat thermometer is used, insert it so that the bulb is in the center of the inside thigh muscle. Be sure the bulb does not touch bone. Cover top and sides of bird with a piece of cheesecloth or thin coarse muslin which has been dipped in melted fat or loosely cover with foil. Do not add water.

Roast at 325°; see timetable for roasting time or until roast meat thermometer registers 190° to 200° F. If cloth dries during roasting, moisten with pan drippings. When ⅔ done, cut string or band of skin between drumsticks and tail. If roasted breast-side down, turn chicken (not turkey) breast-side up to permit breast skin to brown. Remove cloth during last hour of roasting period if the bird is not well browned.

To test for doneness, press thickest part of drumstick between two fingers, protecting fingers with cloth. Meat will feel soft if done and the leg joint will give easily when drumstick is moved up and down.

Chicken rotisseried in your oven or on your barbecue has a delicious flavor. Check your operator's manual for directions.

To bone chicken breasts, start on thickest side and cut along bone to release meat.

OVEN FRIED CHICKEN

  2 lbs. frying chicken, cut into pieces*
  ¾ cup corn flake crumbs
  1½ teaspoons salt
  ¼ teaspoon pepper
  ¼ teaspoon leaf rosemary or ⅛ teaspoon
    poultry seasoning
  1 egg
  1 teaspoon lemon juice

OVEN 350°   6 SERVINGS
                                172 Calories Each

Combine corn flake crumbs, salt, pepper and rosemary. In shallow bowl, combine egg and lemon juice; beat slightly. Dip chicken in egg mixture; then coat with crumb mixture. Place skin-side up in ungreased baking pan. Bake, uncovered, at 350° for 1 to 1¼ hours until chicken is done. (Crumbs adhere best if chicken is not turned during baking.)

Tips: *If desired, use all chicken breasts for lowest calories. Use only ½ cup cornflake crumbs.

To make ahead, coat chicken with crumb mixture early, then refrigerate until ready to bake.

CRANBERRY BAKED CHICKEN

  4 chicken breasts
  Salt
  Pepper
  1½ cups cranberry juice*

OVEN 350°   4 SERVINGS
                                269 Calories Each

Sprinkle chicken with salt and pepper. Place skin-side up in an ungreased baking pan. Pour cranberry juice over chicken. Bake, covered, at 350° for 45 minutes. Uncover; continue baking 30 minutes until brown and tender.

Tips: *For fewer calories, bake chicken in 1½ cups chicken broth or 1½ cups water and 2 cubes chicken bouillon.

Other chicken pieces can be used for the breasts.

Highlight your meal with chicken — marinated for several hours, then grilled, baked or broiled. The flavor is sensational!

BARBECUED CHICKEN

2½ lbs. frying chicken, quartered

OVEN 400°   4 SERVINGS
                             277 Calories Each

Prepare Tomato Barbecue Sauce, page 96 or Spicy Barbecue Sauce, page 97. Set aside. Place chicken in shallow baking dish. Pour sauce over chicken; cover and marinate several hours at room temperature or overnight in refrigerator, turning occasionally. Remove chicken from sauce, reserving marinade for basting sauce; place on broiler pan, skin side up. Bake at 400° for about I hour until tender. (Chicken is done when drumstick twists out of thigh joint readily and the thickest portions are fork tender.) Repeat brushing with sauce every I5 minutes. Do not turn chicken.

Tips: To broil, place chicken skin-side down on broiler pan, 4 to 5 inches from heat. Broil for I5 minutes; brush each piece with I teaspoon sauce. Turn and continue to broil for I5 minutes until tender. Brush occasionally with sauce (additional brushings with sauce will add extra calories).

To grill over hot coals, place chicken on grill, skin-side up. Turn about every I0 minutes, basting with reserved marinade to keep chicken juicy. Grill about 45 minutes until tender.

BROILED CHICKEN

**2½ lbs. frying chicken, cut into pieces
I teaspoon salt
¼ teaspoon pepper
2 tablespoons lemon juice, if desired**

                             6 SERVINGS
                             I6I Calories Each

Place chicken skin-side down on broiler pan 8 to I0 inches from heat. Broil for I0 minutes. Season with salt and pepper. Turn and continue to broil for I5 minutes. Brush occasionally with lemon juice.

ORIENTAL CHICKEN CHOW

      4 chicken breasts
      I teaspoon oil
      ½ cup (I med.) onion wedges
      ½ cup condensed chicken or beef broth*
      ½ cup (5-oz. can) drained bamboo shoots
      ½ cup (5-oz. can) drained and sliced water
          chestnuts
      ¼ cup soy sauce
      I tablespoon sugar
      I tablespoon cornstarch
      I tablespoon cold water
      1½ cups (II-oz. can) drained mandarin
          oranges

4 SERVINGS
316 Calories Each

Brown chicken in hot oil in large fry pan for
7 to I0 minutes. Add onion, broth, bamboo
shoots, water chestnuts and soy sauce. Simmer,
covered, for I5 minutes. Combine sugar and
cornstarch; stir in cold water. Add to chicken
mixture, stirring carefully until mixture
thickens. Add mandarin oranges; heat through.
Serve on rice.

Tips: *If desired, ½ cup water and I bouillon
cube or I teaspoon instant bouillon can be used
for the broth. If desired, bamboo shoots can be
omitted.

Oriental Chicken Chow can be made in an
electric fry pan. Prepare as directed, simmering
at 250°.

For an elegant, company dish, remove bones
from chicken breasts before preparing, page
79. Reduce simmering time to I0 minutes.

Other chicken pieces can be used in this
recipe. White meat has fewer calories, though;
so the weight watcher will want to take a
breast piece.

CHICKEN CREOLE

      2½ lbs. frying chicken, cut into pieces
      I teaspoon cooking oil
      3 cups (20-oz. can) undrained tomatoes
      I cup (I med.) green pepper strips
      ¼ cup (½ med.) onion slices or
          I tablespoon instant minced onion
      I tablespoon parsley flakes
      I teaspoon salt
      ½ teaspoon pepper
      ¼ teaspoon minced garlic
      ¼ teaspoon ground thyme, if desired
      I bay leaf
      I tablespoon cornstarch
      ½ cup water*

6 SERVINGS
I98 Calories Each

Heat oil in large fry pan. Fry chicken until
golden. Drain excess fat. Add tomatoes, green
pepper, onion, parsley, salt, pepper, garlic,
thyme and bay leaf; simmer 30 minutes. Blend
cornstarch with water until smooth. Pour into
fry pan, stirring gently until slightly thickened.
Cover; continue simmering 30 minutes.

Tip: *White wine can be used for the water.

CHICKEN CACCIATORA

      I teaspoon cooking oil
      2½ lbs. frying chicken, cut into pieces
      I cup (2 med.) chopped onions or ¼ cup
          instant minced onion
      ½ teaspoon garlic powder
      I chicken bouillon cube or I teaspoon
          instant chicken bouillon
      I cup boiling water
      2 cups (I-lb. can) undrained tomatoes
      ¾ cup (6-oz. can) tomato paste
      ⅔ cup (6-oz. can) undrained mushrooms
      I tablespoon (3 tsp.) salt
      ½ teaspoon pepper
      ⅛ teaspoon ground thyme
      2 bay leaves
      Dash cayenne pepper

6 SERVINGS
220 Calories Each

Heat oil in large fry pan. Add chicken and
brown until golden. Add onion; brown slightly.
Drain off excess fat. Dissolve bouillon cube
in boiling water. Add to chicken. Add
remaining ingredients. Simmer, covered, for
½ hour. Remove cover and simmer ½ hour
until tender. Serve sauce over chicken.

Try this chicken casserole that features eggplant or okra — two favorite Greek vegetables. For easy eating, bone chicken before cooking, page 99.

GRECIAN CHICKEN

   4 boned chicken breasts*
   I teaspoon salt
   ⅛ teaspoon pepper
   ⅛ teaspoon poultry seasoning or ground thyme, if desired
   I tablespoon parsley flakes or 2 tablespoons chopped parsley
   I tablespoon chopped onion or I teaspoon instant minced onion
   I medium eggplant, peeled and sliced
   2 cups (I-lb. can) tomatoes, drain and reserve ½ cup liquid
   Reserved ½ cup tomato liquid

OVEN 350°   4 SERVINGS
                             257 Calories Each

Place chicken in 2 to 2½-quart casserole. Sprinkle with salt, pepper, poultry seasoning, parsley and onion. Top with eggplant; pour tomatoes and tomato liquid over chicken, breaking tomatoes into smaller pieces. Bake covered at 350° for I hour until chicken is tender.

Tips: *If desired, use I cut-up fryer for chicken breasts. Place in 2½ to 3-quart casserole. Bake 1¼ to 1½ hours.

For flavor variety, 1¾ cups (10-oz. pkg.) frozen cut okra can be broken into small clumps and added to the other ingredients. Or, okra can be used for the eggplant.

CHICKEN BAKE WITH MUSHROOMS

   2½ lbs. chicken, cut into pieces
   I teaspoon salt
   I teaspoon paprika
   ¼ teaspoon pepper
   2 tablespoons cooking oil
   ⅔ cup condensed cream of mushroom soup
   ½ cup (4-oz. can) drained sliced mushrooms

OVEN 350°   6 SERVINGS
                             236 Calories Each

Season chicken with salt, paprika and pepper. Heat oil in large fry pan. Brown chicken on all sides. Place in 13 x 9-inch baking dish or pan. Pour soup over chicken. Bake at 350° for I hour until tender. Sprinkle with mushrooms and return to oven just until hot. If desired, garnish with parsley or paprika.

Tip: Chicken Bake with Mushrooms can be made in a fry pan. Prepare as directed. Simmer, covered, for 45 minutes.

Expand your family's world of eating with this exciting Oriental dish of chicken and vegetables. Served on rice, it only needs a fruit salad to turn it into one of your great successes.

BAMBOO CHICKEN

   6 pieces frying chicken
   I teaspoon butter
   I cup chicken broth*
   2 teaspoons soy sauce
   ½ teaspoon MSG (monosodium glutamate), if desired
   1½ cups (9-oz. pkg.) frozen Chinese pea pods
   ¾ cup (5-oz. can) drained bamboo shoots**
   ½ cup (I stalk) diagonally sliced celery
   I tablespoon cornstarch
   2 tablespoons cold water
   ½ cup (5-oz. can) drained and sliced water chestnuts

                             6 SERVINGS
                             219 Calories Each

In large fry pan, melt butter. Brown chicken well over medium heat. Add broth, soy sauce and MSG; simmer, covered, for 20 minutes. Add pea pods, bamboo shoots and celery; continue simmering 5 minutes until pea pods are tender. Combine cornstarch and cold water; mix well. Drizzle over chicken and vegetables. Continue simmering, stirring gently to blend, until sauce thickens. Add water chestnuts; heat through.

Tips: *If desired, I cup water and I chicken bouillon cube or I teaspoon instant chicken bouillon can be used for the broth.

**If bamboo shoots are not available, ¾ cup additional sliced celery can be used.

If cover is not tight-fitting and liquid evaporates, ¼ cup water can be added to bring amount of liquid to desired level.

GRILLED WIENERS

124 Calories Each

Place wieners crosswise on rack 6 inches above coals. Grill over hot coals for 3 minutes; turn. Cook 5 minutes longer until browned. If desired, brush with barbecue sauce during grilling.

FRANKLY SAUERKRAUT

    1 lb. (8) weiners
  2 cups (1-lb. can) drained sauerkraut
  ¼ cup chopped green pepper
  1 tablespoon brown sugar
  1 tablespoon chopped pimiento, if desired

OVEN 350°   8 SERVINGS
                             139 Calories Each

In ungreased 2 or 2½-quart casserole, combine all ingredients. Bake, covered, at 350° for 20 minutes until heated thoroughly.

Tip: Frankly Sauerkraut can be mixed ahead, covered and refrigerated. When ready to serve, heat as directed.

Wieners in a spicy barbecue sauce. These will be a favorite treat for your children. Easy to make on a hurried evening.

SNAPPY WIENERS

  ¾ lb. (6) wieners
  1½ tablespoons catsup
    1 tablespoon cider vinegar
    1 tablespoon instant minced onion or
    ¼ cup (½ med.) chopped onion
  2 teaspoons Worcestershire sauce
  ¾ teaspoon horseradish, 1 tablespoon
      prepared mustard or 1 teaspoon dry
      mustard

OVEN 350°   6 SERVINGS
                             133 Calories Each

Score wieners diagonally. Place in ungreased 1½-quart baking dish. In small mixing bowl, combine remaining ingredients; mix well. Pour over wieners. Bake, covered, at 350° for 30 minutes. Serve hot.

Tip: To prepare in saucepan, heat over medium heat for 10 to 15 minutes until heated through.

CREOLE LIVER

  ½ teaspoon butter or margarine
  1½ lbs. calf or beef liver, cut into 1½-inch
      strips
  ½ cup (1 med.) chopped onion or
    2 tablespoons instant minced onion
  ¼ cup chopped green pepper
  ½ teaspoon salt
  ⅛ teaspoon leaf marjoram or rosemary
  ⅛ teaspoon ground thyme or poultry
      seasoning
  ¾ cup (6-oz. can) tomato paste
  ½ cup condensed beef consommé*
  ¼ cup water

                             6 SERVINGS
                             182 Calories Each

In large fry pan, brown liver in butter on medium heat. Add remaining ingredients. Simmer, covered, 20 minutes for calf liver or 30 minutes for beef liver, adding small amounts of water if liquid becomes too thick. Serve hot.

Tip: *If desired, ½ cup water, 1 cube or 1 teaspoon beef bouillon and 1 teaspoon Worcestershire sauce can be used for the beef consommé.

LIVER STEAKS

    1 lb. liver, sliced ½ to 1-inch thick
  ¼ teaspoon salt
    Dash pepper

                             4 SERVINGS
                             159 Calories Each

Place liver on broiler pan or cookie sheet. Broil 4 to 5 inches from heat for 3 minutes. Sprinkle with salt and pepper. Turn. Broil second side for 2 to 3 minutes until color just starts to turn. (Do not overcook; liver will toughen.) Cut into individual servings; serve immediately.

Tip: If desired, add one or several of the following to the second side before broiling:

    1 tablespoon bacon-flavored bits
  2 teaspoons chopped onion
    Dash curry powder
  2 tablespoons tomato juice, white wine or
      sherry

Serve this delicious pork roast with green beans and a salad of sliced tomatoes.

PORK LOIN ROAST

4 lbs. center-cut pork loin roast
Salt
Pepper

OVEN 325°   10 SERVINGS
310 Calories Per Slice
(3½ x 2½ x ½-inch)

Have meat man remove backbone from loin. Place roast, fat-side up, on a rack in an open shallow roasting pan. Season with salt and pepper. Insert meat thermometer so the bulb reaches the center thickest part, being sure that the bulb does not rest in fat or on bone. (Do not add water; do not cover.) Roast at 325° for 35 to 40 minutes per pound until thermometer registers 185° F.

CHINESE PORK STRIPS

1 lb. lean pork, cut into ¼-inch strips
¼ teaspoon salt
Dash pepper
½ cup water
½ cup pineapple juice
2 to 3 tablespoons soy sauce
2 cups Chinese cabbage, if desired
1½ cups (7-oz. pkg.) frozen Chinese pea pods
½ cup (5-oz. can) sliced water chestnuts
1 tablespoon cornstarch
1 tablespoon cold water

4 SERVINGS
320 Calories Each

In large fry pan, brown meat over medium high heat. Add ½ cup water, pineapple juice, salt, pepper and soy sauce. Simmer, covered, for 30 minutes. Add Chinese pea pods and water chestnuts. Continue simmering for 10 minutes. Add Chinese cabbage; cover and simmer just until cabbage is tender. Mix cornstarch with 1 tablespoon water. Drizzle over pork mixture, stirring to combine. Heat, stirring carefully, until liquid thickens. Serve over rice.

PORK ROASTS

Pork Loin: A roast from the loin or rib section. (Loin and rib chops are cut from this section.) Sometimes sold boned and rolled.

Fresh Ham: The same cut as ham only it hasn't been cured and smoked, so it tastes like a Pork Roast. Makes a nice roast for a large group. Carve like you would ham.

Shoulder Roasts: Would include: Arm Roast, Blade Roast or Boston Shoulder Roast, as well as Boneless Rolled Roast. Makes a tender roast but contains bone (unless boned) and more fat than a Loin Roast.

CHOPS

Loin and Rib Chops: Chops from the loin-rib area. Loin chops have the tenderloin on one side of the bone; rib chops have no tenderloin. These are sometimes cured and smoked and sold as smoked pork chops.

Shoulder: Sometimes referred to as arm or blade chops or steaks. These chops are from the shoulder area so contain more smaller muscles than rib chops.

PORK TENDERLOIN

The piece of tenderloin is sometimes removed and sold separately. Like in beef, this is considered the most tender cut of pork.

SMOKED PICNIC SHOULDER

Picnic always refers to shoulder area. When cured and smoked, it tastes like smoked ham, but is less expensive because there is more bone and waste and it is harder to carve.

Seasonings, Spices and Herbs for Pork:

Tabasco sauce, horseradish, soy sauce, tomato sauce, Worcestershire sauce, chili sauce, garlic, herb or wine vinegar, mustard, allspice, caraway, celery seed, chili powder, cinnamon, ground cloves, whole cloves, rosemary, sage, tarragon, thyme, basil, dill, oregano.

BRAISED PORK CHOPS

6 rib, loin or shoulder pork chops, cut
   ¾ to 1-inch thick
½ teaspoon salt
⅛ teaspoon pepper
¼ cup water*

Brown chops on both sides in large fry pan. Season with salt and pepper; add water. Cover; simmer 45 to 60 minutes until tender.

Tip: *To vary flavor, use different fruit or vegetable juices for the water — orange, pineapple, tomato.

This hearty meat pie is almost a complete meal. It can be a nifty disguise for a veal roast you had a few days ago. Add coleslaw or a salad to round out your meal.

SHEPHERD'S PIE

I½ lbs. boneless veal, cut into I-inch cubes
I teaspoon oil or shortening
I chicken bouillon cube or I teaspoon instant bouillon*
I½ cups boiling water
½ teaspoon soy sauce
¼ cup (I med.) chopped onion or I tablespoon instant minced onion
2 tablespoons flour
I teaspoon salt
⅛ teaspoon pepper
⅛ teaspoon curry powder
¼ cup water
I¾ cups (I0-oz. pkg.) frozen mixed vegetables
2 cups mashed potatoes, page I08

OVEN 400°   4 SERVINGS
                                   4I4 Calories Each

In large fry pan, brown meat on all sides in oil. Add bouillon, I½ cups water, soy sauce and onion to fry pan. In cup or small bowl, mix flour, salt, pepper, curry powder and ¼ cup water together. Gradually stir into meat mixture. Cover tightly and simmer I hour until tender. Stir occasionally. Add frozen mixed vegetables and stir until vegetables separate. Pour into ungreased 2 to 2½-quart casserole. Top with mashed potatoes, using a fork or pastry tube. Bake, uncovered, at 400° for 20 minutes until potatoes are lightly browned.

Tips: *If desired, I½ cups chicken broth can be used for the bouillon cube and water.

To use leftover veal roast, 4 cups cubed cooked veal can be used for the fresh. Do not brown meat. Prepare recipe as directed, simmering only until mixture thickens. Bake as directed.

To make ahead, prepare meat and vegetable mixture as directed. Top with mashed potatoes. Cool, cover and refrigerate. Bake, uncovered, at 400° for 25 to 30 minutes until potatoes are lightly browned.

Start with chow mein meat or equal parts of pork and veal cut into small, thin strips. Serve with a fruit salad in 45 minutes.

CHOW MEIN

I lb. chow mein meat
I tablespoon oil or shortening
I cup (8 oz. or ½ pt.) sliced fresh mushrooms
I medium onion, sliced
I cup (2 stalks) sliced celery
½ teaspoon salt
½ teaspoon ground ginger
3 tablespoons soy sauce
I bouillon cube or I teaspoon instant bouillon
I cup water
2 cups (I-lb. can) drained bean sprouts
⅔ cup (5-oz. can) sliced, drained water chestnuts
½ cup (5-oz. can) drained bamboo shoots
I tablespoon cornstarch
2 tablespoons water

                                    4 SERVINGS
                                   308 Calories Each

In fry pan, brown meat in hot oil. Add mushrooms and onion; brown slightly. Add celery, salt, ginger, soy sauce, bouillon and I cup water. Cover and simmer 20 minutes. Add bean sprouts, water chestnuts and bamboo shoots. Combine cornstarch with 2 tablespoons water. Stir into meat mixture; bring to boil, stirring constantly. Cover and simmer I5 more minutes. Serve over rice.

Tips: Two cups (I-lb. can) drained chow mein vegetables can be used for bean sprouts, water chestnuts and bamboo shoots.

For crisper vegetables, add onion and celery when bean sprouts are added.

For Beef Chow Mein, use I lb. beef sirloin, cut into I-inch pieces. Prepare as directed.

Less tender cuts of beef can also be used. Marinate for 3 to 4 hours in I teaspoon MSG, ½ cup water and ½ cup soy sauce. Drain well. Prepare as directed.

LEG OF LAMB

The back leg section of the lamb. Available whole or cut into smaller sections. Also available boned.

Seasonings, Spices and Herbs for Lamb:

Tabasco sauce, chili sauce, garlic, herb or wine vinegar, curry powder, mace, pepper, allspice, peppermint, sage, spearmint, tarragon, thyme, basil, bay leaf, chervil, dill, marjoram, mint.

LEG OF LAMB
OVEN 325°

235 Calories Per Slice
(3½ x 3 x ½-inch)

Place leg of lamb skin-side down on rack in open shallow roasting pan. Season with salt and pepper. Insert meat thermometer so the bulb reaches the center of the thickest part of the leg, being sure the bulb does not rest in fat or on bone. (Do not add water; do not cover.) Roast at 325° to desired degree of doneness, adding one of the glazes during roasting, if desired.

Timetable for Roasting

Weight	Meat Thermometer Reading	Approx. Cooking Time per lb.
5 to 8 lbs.	165 to 170°	25 to 30 min.
3 to 5 lbs.	165 to 170°	25 to 30 min.

MINTED LEG OF LAMB: Rub roast with 1 teaspoon mint leaves before roasting.

GARLIC GLAZE FOR LEG OF LAMB: Combine ⅓ cup dry sherry, ⅓ cup water, 1 tablespoon paprika, ½ teaspoon leaf basil, 2 tablespoons soy sauce and 3 cloves garlic, minced; brush meat with glaze every 15 minutes during roasting.

SPICY GLAZE FOR LEG OF LAMB: Combine 2 tablespoons brown sugar, 1 clove garlic, minced, 2 teaspoons salt, ½ teaspoon dry mustard, ½ teaspoon chili powder, ¼ teaspoon ground ginger, ¼ teaspoon ground cloves and 1 tablespoon lemon juice. Spread over meat during last 30 to 60 minutes of roasting.

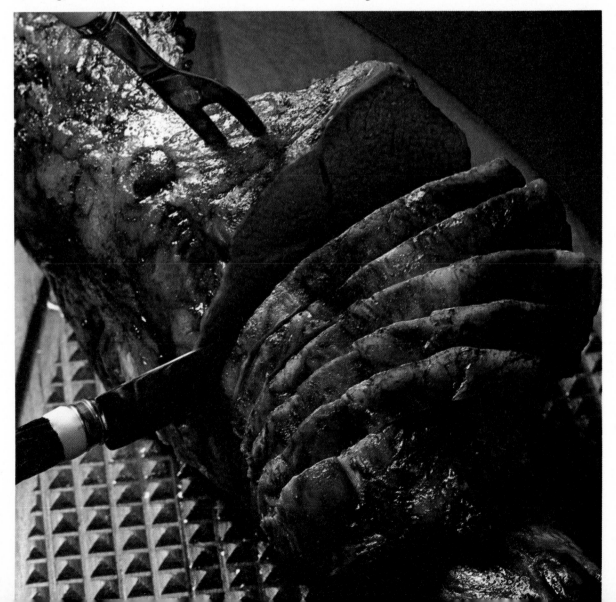

SOUTH SEAS LAMB CHOPS

   I teaspoon salt
   2 tablespoons soy sauce
   2 tablespoons grated orange peel
   ⅓ cup orange juice
   6 shoulder lamb chops, cut I-inch thick

6 SERVINGS
200 Calories Each

Combine all ingredients except chops in shallow pan. Place chops in pan and marinate 2 hours, turning after I hour. Arrange chops on broiler rack. Place under broiler, 2 to 3 inches from heat. Broil 8 to I0 minutes until brown. Turn, brush with marinade and broil other side 6 to 8 minutes until brown.

Tip: Try this marinade on other lamb chops — rib or loin.

Try lamb shoulder chops braised in a savory mushroom sauce. Serve with peas and a fruit salad.

BRAISED LAMB CHOPS

   4 lamb shoulder chops
   I teaspoon oil or shortening
   ½ teaspoon salt
   ⅛ teaspoon pepper
   ⅛ teaspoon garlic powder or instant
      minced garlic
   ⅔ cup (4-oz. can) undrained mushroom
      stems and pieces
   2 tablespoons flour
   ½ cup water

4 SERVINGS
I79 Calories Each

In large fry pan, brown chops in oil on both sides. Season with salt, pepper and garlic powder. Add mushrooms. Cover; simmer 45 to 60 minutes until tender. Remove chops to warm platter. Combine flour with water; add to liquid in pan. Cook, stirring constantly, until mixture boils and thickens; serve over chops.

STEW AND RIBLETS

Lean, meaty squares for use in stews. Sometimes lamb riblets are sold as stew meat — these contain tip of rib bones and rib cartilage.

LAMB STEW

   I½ lbs. lamb meat
   I teaspoon MSG (monosodium glutamate),
      if desired
   ½ teaspoon salt
   ½ teaspoon ground marjoram or thyme,
      if desired
   ¼ teaspoon pepper
   2 cubes beef bouillon or 2 teaspoons
      instant beef bouillon
   I clove garlic or ¼ teaspoon garlic powder
      or I teaspoon garlic salt
   I bay leaf
   I cup white wine or water
   2 cups water
   2 cups (4 med.) carrot pieces, cut into
      2-inch pieces
   I cup (2 med.) onion wedges
   2 tablespoons flour
   2 tablespoons water

4 SERVINGS
359 Calories Each

Brown lamb in large fry pan or Dutch oven over medium high heat. Add MSG, salt, marjoram, pepper, bouillon, garlic, bay leaf, wine and 2 cups water. Simmer, covered, for I hour. Add carrots and onion; simmer, covered, for 30 to 45 minutes until tender. Remove bay leaf. Combine flour and 2 tablespoons water; add to stew mixture. Bring to boil to thicken.

Tips: Lamb Stew can be prepared as directed in an electric fry pan.

Lamb Stew can be made ahead. Simmer for I hour; cool, cover and refrigerate or freeze. Before reheating, skim off any visible fat. Add vegetables and simmer for about I hour until meat and vegetables are tender.

OVEN FRIED FISH

   I lb. perch fillets*
   ½ teaspoon salt
   Dash pepper
   I egg, slightly beaten
   I tablespoon lemon juice
   ½ to ¾ cup crushed corn flakes

OVEN 350°   4 SERVINGS
I45 Calories Each

In shallow bowl, combine egg, lemon juice, salt and pepper; mix well. Dip fish in egg mixture, then in crumbs. Place in ungreased baking dish. Bake, uncovered, at 350° for 20 to 25 minutes until fish flakes easily.

Tip: *Other fish fillets (cod, halibut, flounder, haddock) can be used for the perch.

Time was when you had to be within distance of a seashore to know the taste of lobster, and fresh-water fish appeared on the table only when luck was with the angler. Today the wonders of the ocean are within reach of your shopping cart.

Frozen fish — whole, steaks or fillets — are ready to cook; shrimp or scallops can be purchased frozen or already cooked. Be sure you buy them solidly frozen and keep them that way until ready to prepare. Thaw them in the refrigerator or, if short on time, under cold running water. Drain, pat dry and cook immediately. Several varieties of fresh water fish are also available frozen; and salmon, tuna, lobster, shrimp and crab are long-time canned favorites.

Fresh fish and seafood should be firm and elastic, leaving no imprint of the finger when pressed. Gills should be bright red, eyes bright and bulging, and fish should not have a strong odor. Fresh lobsters and crabs should be purchased alive, and oysters and clams should be tightly closed when purchased.

Store fish wrapped in foil or waxed paper in a tightly covered container in the coldest part of the refrigerator. Wash and dry thoroughly before cooking. When thawed, use the same day or the next.

Seasonings, Spices and Herbs for Fish:

Tabasco sauce, lemon juice, tomato sauce, Worcestershire sauce, garlic, mustard, paprika, pepper, parsley, thyme, tarragon, bay leaf, marjoram.

BROILED FISH

    I lb. fish fillets or steaks
    Salt
    Pepper
    I tablespoon butter or margarine, melted

BROIL   4 SERVINGS
                  125 Calories Each

Cut fish into serving pieces, if desired. Sprinkle with salt and pepper. Place fish on broiler pan. Broil until golden brown. Distance from heat and broiling time depend on cut and thickness of the fish.

For fillets about ¼ to I-inch thick — place 2 inches from heat and broil 5 to 8 minutes.

For steaks about ½ to I-inch thick — place 2 to 3 inches from heat and broil I0 to I2 minutes, turning once after 5 minutes.

Place on hot platter and serve with lemon wedges. If desired, garnish with parsley sprigs.

CHEESE-TOPPED FILLETS

    I lb. pike fillets*
    ½ teaspoon salt
    ½ teaspoon MSG (monosodium glutamate), if desired
    I tablespoon flour
    ¼ teaspoon paprika
    ¼ teaspoon garlic salt
    4 slices (2 oz.) American cheese

OVEN 400°   4 SERVINGS
                 I58 Calories Each

In shallow baking pan, sprinkle fish with salt, MSG, flour, paprika and garlic salt. Sprinkle with flour; top with paprika. Bake at 400° for I5 to 20 minutes, until fish flakes. Top with cheese; place under broiler until cheese bubbles.

Tip: *Other fillets such as perch, turbot, sole, haddock or halibut can be used for the pike.

INDIVIDUAL BAKED FILLETS

    I lb. turbot, sole, haddock or halibut fillets
    I tablespoon butter or margarine
    ½ cup (4-oz. can) drained mushroom stems and pieces
    ¼ cup finely chopped green onions
    I tablespoon minced parsley or I teaspoon parsley flakes
    I teaspoon salt
    ¼ teaspoon MSG (monosodium glutamate), if desired
    ⅛ teaspoon pepper
    I teaspoon lemon peel
    2 tablespoons flour
    I cup skim milk
    Dash paprika
    Heavy foil

OVEN 400°   4 SERVINGS
                 I75 Calories Each

Melt butter in fry pan; sauté mushrooms and onions 5 to I0 minutes until moisture is cooked away. Blend in parsley, salt, MSG, pepper, lemon peel and flour. Add milk; cook over medium heat, stirring constantly, until mixture thickens. Cut foil into six I8x9-inch pieces. Divide half of the mushroom mixture into 6 portions, spooning one portion onto center of each piece of foil. Place fish on sauce; top with remaining sauce. Bring edges of foil together, seal top and ends with double folds. Place seam-side up on cookie sheet or shallow baking pan. Bake at 400° for 30 to 40 minutes until fish flakes. Serve immediately.

This flavorful loaf is a favorite of fish-lovers. Easy to make, it bakes in only 40 minutes. Serve with broccoli and a molded salad.

SALMON LOAF

> 2 cups (I-lb. can) drained salmon
> I cup soft bread cubes
> 2 eggs, slightly beaten
> 2 tablespoons minced parsley
> I teaspoon grated lemon peel
> ½ teaspoon salt
> ⅛ teaspoon ground thyme, if desired
> ⅛ teaspoon pepper
> ½ cup water

OVEN 350°   6 SERVINGS
                                214 Calories Each

Flake salmon in a bowl; remove bones and skin. Add remaining ingredients; blend well. Place in greased 8x4-inch loaf pan. Set in pan containing I-inch hot water; bake at 350° for 30 to 40 minutes.

Tip: I cup cracker crumbs can be used for the soft bread cubes.

CREAMED TUNA

> ½ cup skim milk
> ½ cup condensed cream of celery soup
> 1½ cups (two 6½-oz. cans) well-drained tuna chunks
> Dash paprika

                    4 (½ cup) SERVINGS
                        188 Calories Each

In medium saucepan, combine milk and soup. Add tuna chunks; stir lightly to coat. Simmer over low heat until heated through. Serve over rice; sprinkle with paprika. If desired, garnish with parsley or lemon slices.

MARINATED HALIBUT

> 12-oz. halibut fillets or steaks
> I teaspoon salt
> ¼ to ½ teaspoon paprika
> ½ cup (I med.) chopped onion
> 3 tablespoons lemon juice

BROIL   4 SERVINGS
                                 78 Calories Each

Sprinkle halibut with salt and paprika. Place halibut in shallow pan or bowl. Sprinkle with onion and lemon juice. Cover; let stand I hour (turning after ½ hour). Drain and reserve liquid. Broil on ungreased broiler pan 4 inches

from heat for 5 minutes on each side, basting with reserved liquid during broiling. Serve hot.

Tip: For variety, add ¼ cup chopped green pepper with the onion.

Swordfish with a hint of lemon. Add baked potatoes, a vegetable salad and a fruity dessert for a satisfying meal. Note the tip for a fun idea!

BROILED MARINATED SWORDFISH

> ¼ cup lemon juice
> I teaspoon grated onion
> 2 lbs. swordfish steaks, cut ½-inch thick
> Salt
> Pepper
> 2 tablespoons minced parsley

BROIL   6 SERVINGS
                                182 Calories Each

Combine lemon juice and onion. Marinate swordfish in mixture for I hour. Drain. Place on broiler pan. Broil about 3 inches from heat for 5 to 8 minutes on each side, until fish flakes. Season with salt and pepper. Sprinkle with parsley before serving.

BROILED SALMON STEAKS

> ¾ lb. (2 large) salmon steaks
> I teaspoon parsley flakes
> ½ teaspoon salt
> Dash pepper
> 2 tablespoons lemon juice*

BROIL   4 SERVINGS
                                187 Calories Each

Sprinkle salmon with parsley flakes, salt and pepper. In shallow bowl or pan, add lemon juice. Marinate for I hour, turning after 30 minutes. Place steaks on ungreased broiler pan; broil 8 to 10 inches from heat for 5 minutes on each side. Salmon should flake easily when pierced with fork. Serve with lemon.

Tips: *Extra dry vermouth can be used for the lemon juice.

Salmon steaks can be baked, covered, at 325° for 20 minutes. Add 2 tablespoons chopped onion or I teaspoon instant minced onion to lemon juice; do not drain juice before baking.

Seasonings, Spices and Herbs for Seafood:

Lemon juice, cayenne, garlic, mustard, paprika, pepper, parsley, thyme, bay leaf, chives.

SWEET-SOUR SHRIMP

- ¾ cup water-packed pineapple tidbits or chunks, drained, reserve liquid
  Reserved 1 cup pineapple liquid (add water if necessary)
- ½ cup white or cider vinegar
- ¼ cup hot water
- 2 chicken bouillon cubes or 2 teaspoons instant bouillon
- 1 teaspoon paprika
- ½ teaspoon prepared mustard
  Dash pepper
- 3½ cups (12-oz. pkg.) unthawed frozen medium shrimp*
- ½ cup (1 med.) green pepper chunks
- ½ cup (1 stalk) diagonally sliced celery
- ½ cup (1 med.) sliced onion or 2 tablespoons instant minced onion
- 2 tablespoons cornstarch
- ⅓ cup sugar

6 SERVINGS
139 Calories Each

In large saucepan, combine pineapple liquid vinegar, ¼ cup water, bouillon cubes, paprika, mustard and pepper. Cook over low heat until bouillon cubes are dissolved. Reserve ¼ cup sauce. Add shrimp to saucepan; simmer 10 minutes. Add pineapple tidbits, green pepper, celery and sliced onion; cook 3 minutes until vegetables are crisp, but tender. Combine cornstarch, sugar and reserved ¼ cup sauce; mix well. Stir into shrimp mixture; cook about 2 minutes until clear and thickened. Serve hot.

Tips: *Fresh or canned shrimp can be used for the frozen.

For Sweet-Sour Meatballs combine 1 lb. lean ground beef with 1 teaspoon salt. Shape into 24 meatballs, about 1¼-inch balls. In medium fry pan, brown meatballs. Drain thoroughly. Follow directions above using beef bouillon cubes instead of chicken, simmering in liquid and continuing as directed.

93

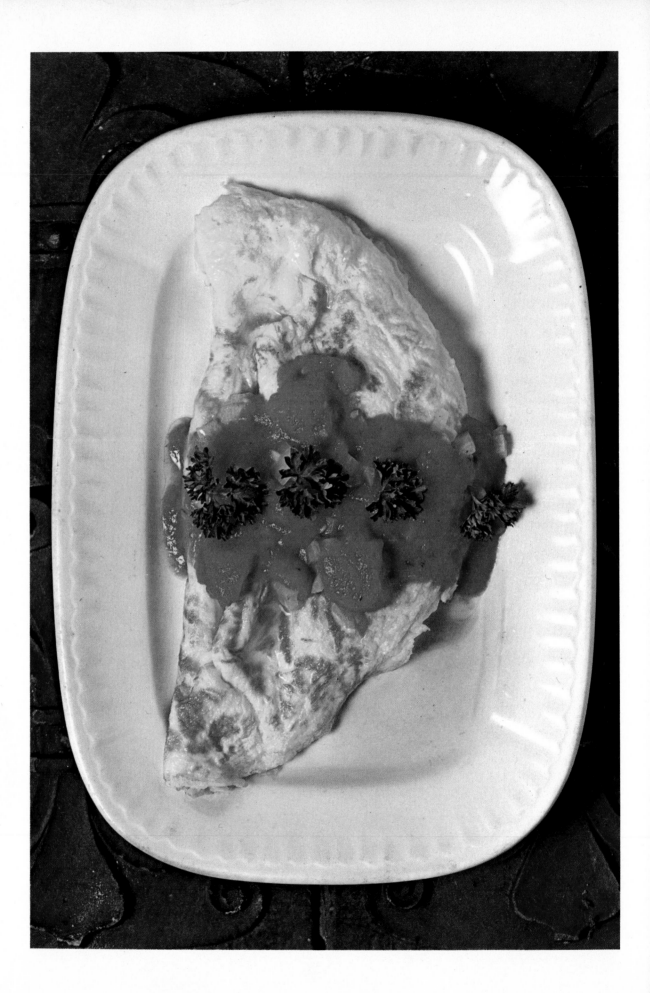

Eggs are for every day or elegance; they are prized for their nutritive value. For this reason eggs offer a quick solution to breakfast, lunch or supper as the feature or as a nutritious garnish. Pair them with mushrooms, seafood, fish, curry, turkey, cheese, paprika, pimiento, parsley, chives, tarragon or watercress.

The color of eggs has nothing to do with quality, but depends merely on the breed of hen. Brown or white eggs come in all sizes and grades and are identical in nutritional value.

Eggs are graded AA (Fancy), A, B and C, and the difference is seen in the spread of the egg white when they are broken. Eggs may also be marketed as jumbo, extra large, large, medium and small, depending on their size. The size of eggs has nothing to do with their quality. All sizes can be purchased in all grades. Small eggs are an economical buy if they are at least one-fourth less expensive than large eggs; medium, if they are one-eighth less expensive than the large size.

Go Spanish with this yummy dish that can be served for breakfast, lunch or supper. Serve with the appropriate side dishes. Olé!

SPANISH OMELET

  ½ cup (I med.) finely chopped onion or
    2 tablespoons instant minced onion
  I tablespoon butter or margarine
  I tablespoon flour
I½ cups drained, chopped, canned or fresh
    tomatoes
  ½ teaspoon salt
  ½ teaspoon cream-style horseradish
  ¼ teaspoon pepper
  I recipe French Omelet

4 SERVINGS
190 Calories Each

Sauté onion in butter in fry pan until tender. Blend in flour. Add remaining ingredients for sauce. Simmer, stirring occasionally, about 20 minutes until mixture thickens slightly. Prepare omelet. Spoon part of tomato mixture on half of omelet before folding. Turn out onto plate; top with remaining sauce.

To keep hard-cooked eggs from getting dark around the yolk, bring to a boil, then reduce heat and simmer for 15 minutes. Immediately immerse in cold water.

FRENCH OMELET

  2 tablespoons butter or margarine
  4 eggs
  ¼ cup skim milk
  ¼ teaspoon salt
  Dash pepper

4 SERVINGS
134 Calories Each

Melt butter in fry pan over low to medium heat. Beat eggs, milk and seasonings until blended; pour into fry pan. Keep heat low and lift edges of omelet as it cooks, allowing uncooked eggs to flow to bottom of fry pan until entire mixture is cooked. Do not stir. To fold, quickly loosen omelet around edges. Slip spatula or pancake turner under one side and fold omelet in half. Tilt the fry pan and roll out onto plate.

Tip: You don't need a special omelet pan to make an omelet. A heavy fry pan is best. A dark cast-iron fry pan makes darker crust; light-colored metal, a lighter crust. The fry pan for an omelet must be completely smooth to prevent the egg from sticking.

ORIENTAL OMELET

  I tablespoon butter or margarine
  2 tablespoons finely chopped onion or
    I teaspoon instant minced onion
  I tablespoon finely chopped green pepper,
    if desired
  ½ cup drained bean sprouts
  ½ teaspoon soy sauce
  ⅛ teaspoon ground ginger
  I recipe French Omelet

4 SERVINGS
165 Calories Each

Melt butter in fry pan over low heat; sauté onion and green pepper in butter. Add remaining ingredients for filling; heat. Prepare omelet. Spoon half of mixture on half of omelet; fold. Turn out onto plate; top with remaining mixture.

Tip: For heartier Oriental Omelet, add ½ cup chopped cleaned shrimp to filling.

EGGS SUISSE

I tablespoon butter or margarine
4 eggs
¼ cup skim milk
Salt
Pepper
¼ cup shredded Swiss cheese

OVEN 350°   4 SERVINGS
                        135 Calories Each

Brush 4 custard cups with butter. Break I egg into each cup; top each with I tablespoon of the milk. Season with salt and pepper. Bake at 350° for I5 minutes until eggs are set. Sprinkle cheese over eggs. Continue baking for 5 minutes until cheese melts.

For a weekend breakfast, try this attractive way of serving eggs. Your children might enjoy making this dish for breakfast.

EGGS BAKED IN TOAST CUPS

4 thin slices fresh bread
2 tablespoons soft butter or margarine
4 eggs

OVEN 350°   4 SERVINGS
                        190 Calories Each

Trim crusts from bread; brush both sides of each slice with butter. Fit gently into 3-inch muffin tins. Bake at 350° for I0 to I5 minutes until lightly browned. Break one egg into each toast cup. Continue baking for I5 to 20 minutes until eggs are set. Season to taste with salt and pepper.

SCRAMBLED EGGS

4 eggs
¼ cup skim milk
¼ teaspoon salt
Dash pepper
2 tablespoons butter or margarine

                        3 SERVINGS
                        178 Calories Each

In small bowl, combine egg, milk and seasonings. Melt butter in fry pan over low heat. Pour eggs into fry pan and stir from outside edge toward center, allowing uncooked egg in center to flow to outside. Continue stirring until all the egg has cooked and has a creamy appearance.

Tips: Double recipe for 6 servings.

Scrambled eggs will be a clear golden yellow if: butter is not allowed to brown, pan is a light color, heat is kept low to medium. Scrambled eggs may be dark if: bacon has been cooked in the pan first, pan is a dark color, heat is too high, butter is allowed to brown.

A dieter's treat, keep this tomatoey sauce on hand to marinate and to brush on favorite meats, such as hamburgers and chicken.

TOMATO BARBECUE SAUCE

½ cup cold water
½ cup (I med.) chopped onion or
    2 tablespoons instant minced onion
¼ cup catsup
2 tablespoons vinegar
I teaspoon salt
¼ cup sugar
I teaspoon Worcestershire sauce
I teaspoon prepared mustard
¼ teaspoon pepper

                        I CUP SAUCE
                        I9 Calories Per Tablespoon

In small mixing bowl, combine all ingredients; mix well. Store in refrigerator. Use as a marinade and to brush on hamburgers, chicken and other meats.

Here's a low calorie way to make gravy. Remove all fat from your meat juices to insure the lowest number of calories.

LOW CALORIE GRAVY

I cup water*
3 tablespoons instant nonfat dry milk
I tablespoon flour
I tablespoon meat juice or ½ teaspoon
    Kitchen Bouquet
⅛ teaspoon salt
Dash pepper
I bouillon cube or I teaspoon instant
    bouillon

                        I CUP
                        4 Calories Per Tablespoon

In small saucepan, combine all ingredients; mix well. Cook over low heat, stirring constantly, until mixture thickens slightly and comes to a boil. Simmer for 5 minutes.

Tip: *If desired, I cup beef or chicken broth can be used for the water. Omit salt and bouillon cube.

This unusual sauce will give meats a spicy note that will tempt your family and guests for "seconds". Make it ahead to have on hand.

SPICY BARBECUE SAUCE

    ½ teaspoon cinnamon
    ½ teaspoon ground ginger
    ½ teaspoon ground nutmeg
    ½ teaspoon paprika
    ¼ teaspoon garlic salt
    2 tablespoons sugar
    ¼ cup (½ med.) chopped onion or I table-
        spoon instant minced onion
    I cup water

I CUP SAUCE
7 Calories Per Tablespoon

In small mixing bowl, combine all ingredients; mix well. Store in refrigerator. Use as a marinade and to brush on hamburgers and other meats.

Let this tasty sauce simmer by itself for several hours. Reheat before serving for a convenient meal.

SPAGHETTI SAUCE

    I teaspoon cooking oil
    ½ cup (I med.) chopped onion or
        2 tablespoons instant minced onion
    I clove garlic, crushed, or ¼ teaspoon
        minced garlic
    3 cups (I-lb. I2-oz. can) undrained
        tomatoes*
    I½ cups (two 6-oz. cans) tomato paste
    I½ teaspoons salt
    I teaspoon leaf oregano, Italian seasoning
        or basil
    I teaspoon parsley flakes
    ¼ teaspoon pepper

9 (½ cup) SERVINGS
53 Calories Each

In large saucepan, brown onion and garlic in oil. (If instant minced onion and garlic are used, omit oil; add them directly to tomatoes.) Add remaining ingredients; mix well. Simmer, covered, 2 hours until flavors have blended. Serve over spaghetti.

Tips: *A I-lb. can and an 8-oz. can tomatoes can be used for the I-lb. I2-oz. can.

For Spaghetti Sauce with Meatballs, prepare Spaghetti Sauce as directed. Combine I lb. lean ground beef with I teaspoon salt. Form into balls. Brown in large fry pan. Drain well, using paper towel to absorb all fat. Add meatballs to sauce. Continue simmering 30 minutes.

Spaghetti Sauce can be doubled. If desired, freeze portions for convenience on a busy day.

Use this basic Cream Sauce as a reduced calorie base for your favorite sauces. Note tips for some variations we suggest.

CREAM SAUCE

    2 tablespoons flour
    2 tablespoons instant nonfat dry milk
    I teaspoon seasoned salt or salt
    ½ teaspoon MSG (monosodium glutamate),
        if desired
    ¼ teaspoon salt
    Dash pepper
    I¼ cups cold water

I¼ CUPS SAUCE
4 Calories Per Tablespoon

In small saucepan, combine all ingredients except water; mix well. Add water slowly, stirring well. Cook over medium heat, stirring constantly, until mixture thickens and comes to a boil. Serve.

Tips: For Creamy Gravy, I to 4 tablespoons meat juices or ½ teaspoon Kitchen Bouquet can be added after the water.

For extra flavor, I bouillon cube, dissolved in ¼ cup hot water, can be added after the water; omit salt and reduce water to I cup.

To use skim milk, add I¼ cups skim milk to flour mixture; omit instant nonfat dry milk and water.

For Zesty Cheese Sauce, use regular salt; add ¼ cup grated Cheddar or American cheese and dash Worcestershire sauce to thickened mixture. Stir until cheese is melted.

Leftovers can be stored, covered, in refrigerator for about I week. Reheat for reuse.

Vegetables

ASPARAGUS

Amount to purchase for 4 servings:
1½ lbs. spears, (about 30 spears).
1 lb. tips, (2 cups).

Peak season: Early spring.

Look for: Stalks should be green and tender. The tips should be dark green and close to the stalk. The buds on the tip will spread, after they have been cut.

Basic preparation: Trim 1 inch from stalk end. Wash thoroughly in cold water.

Storage: Fresh asparagus spears should be wrapped in an airtight container and stored in the crisper or lower part of the refrigerator 1 to 2 days.

Cooking time and method: Cook in small amount of water, loosely covered.
Boil spears: 10 to 20 minutes.
Boil tips: 5 to 10 minutes.
Steam spears: 12 to 30 minutes.
Steam tips: 7 to 10 minutes.
Pressure cook spears: ½ to 1½ minutes.
Pressure cook tips: ½ to 2 minutes.

Source of vitamins A & C.

Seasonings, Spices and Herbs: Tabasco sauce, lemon juice, nutmeg, paprika, pepper, parsley, thyme, bay leaf, marjoram.

ASPARAGUS DELIGHT

  ½ cup water
  1 tablespoon chopped onion or
    ½ teaspoon instant minced onion
  1 tablespoon chopped green pepper
  1 teaspoon chopped pimiento, if desired
  ½ teaspoon salt
    Dash pepper
1½ cups (10-oz. pkg.) frozen asparagus
    spears or cut asparagus
  1 teaspoon tarragon vinegar or cider
    vinegar

4 SERVINGS
16 Calories Each

In medium saucepan, bring water, onion, green pepper, pimiento, salt and pepper to a boil. Add asparagus; bring to a boil. Simmer, covered, for 5 to 8 minutes until tender. Drain. Sprinkle with vinegar. Serve.

Tip: If desired, 2 cups (1-lb. can) undrained cut asparagus or asparagus spears can be used for the frozen. Omit water; combine all ingredients in saucepan; simmer over medium heat until heated through.

Broccoli topped with mustard and dill seed makes a colorful and delicious vegetable. A great accompaniment for beef or pork.

BROCCOLI MOUTARDE

1¾ cups (10 oz. pkg.) frozen broccoli spears
    or chopped broccoli
  1 tablespoon prepared mustard
  ¼ teaspoon dill seed, if desired

4 SERVINGS
23 Calories Each

Prepare broccoli as directed on package. Drain, Drizzle mustard and sprinkle dill seed over spears. Serve hot.

BROCCOLI

Amount to purchase for 4 servings:
1½ lbs.

Peak season: All year.

Look for: Stalks should be firm and tender with green flowerettes. Flowerettes should be tightly closed. Yellow flowerettes are inferior quality.

Basic preparation: Wash carefully in cold water. Remove large outer leaves and tough part of stalk. Wash thoroughly. For quicker cooking, make slits lengthwise into thick stalk up to flowerettes. Or, stalk can be cut from flowerettes and sliced.

Storage: Place in airtight container and refrigerate 4 to 5 days.

Cooking time and method: Cook in small amount of water, loosely covered.
Boil: 10 to 15 minutes.
Steam: 15 to 20 minutes.
Pressure cook: 1½ to 2 minutes.

Source of vitamins A & C.

Seasonings, Spices and Herbs: Tabasco sauce, lemon juice, garlic, nutmeg, pepper, caraway, ground cloves, parsley, tarragon, thyme, bay leaf.

To hasten cooking of the thick stalks of asparagus or broccoli, tie the vegetables in a bundle and stand upright in a large pan with water. Cover so that thick stalks cook in water, while the tender tops are steamed. Thus, the stalks become tender while the tops are not overcooked.

BEANS

Amount to purchase for 4 servings:
1½ lbs., (4½ cups)

Peak season: Summer.

Look for: Pods should be clean, firm and free of blemishes.

Basic preparation: Wash and break off ends. Leave whole, break into pieces or slice lengthwise.

Storage: Place in crisper of refrigerator or wrap and store in lower part of refrigerator for 3 to 5 days.

Cooking time and method: Cook in small amount of water, tightly covered.
Boil: 15 to 20 minutes.
Steam: 20 to 25 minutes.
Pressure cook: 1½ to 2 minutes.

Source of vitamins A & C.

Seasonings, Spices and Herbs: Lemon juice, garlic, mustard, nutmeg, pepper, caraway, rosemary, thyme, basil, bay leaf, dill, mint, oregano.

Wax beans dressed up with a sauce and dotted with green pepper and pimiento. Colorful and good!

CONFETTI WAX BEANS

1½ cups (9-oz. pkg.) cooked and drained
    frozen wax beans
¼ cup chopped green pepper
2 tablespoons chopped pimiento
2 tablespoons plain yogurt

        3 (½ cup) SERVINGS
        39 Calories Each

In small saucepan, combine all ingredients; mix lightly. Heat through.

Tips: A combination of wax beans and green beans can be used. Calories will vary accordingly.

If desired, 2 cups (1-lb. can) drained wax beans can be used for the frozen beans. Prepare as directed.

To make ahead, prepare as directed, placing cooked beans in a 1-quart casserole. Cover and refrigerate; reheat, covered, at 350° for 20 to 25 minutes until heated through.

Celery is sautéed in butter to give a rich flavor to green beans. Ready to serve in only 20 minutes!

SUPREME GREEN BEANS

1 tablespoon butter or margarine
½ cup (1 med. stalk) sliced celery
2 cups (1-lb. can) drained green beans
1 teaspoon salt
   Dash pepper

        4 (½ cup) SERVINGS
        42 Calories Each

In medium saucepan, sauté celery in butter over medium heat about 10 minutes until celery is tender. Add beans, salt and pepper; toss lightly. Heat through.

Tip: If desired, 1¾ cups (10-oz. pkg.) cooked and drained frozen green beans can be used for the canned green beans.

ITALIAN BEANS AND ONIONS

1¾ cups (10-oz. pkg.) frozen Italian beans
1 cup (8½-oz. can) drained white onions
⅛ teaspoon Italian seasoning or oregano
⅓ cup tomato juice

        4 (½ cup) SERVINGS
        41 Calories Each

Prepare beans as directed on package, adding onions and seasoning with beans. Drain. Stir in tomato juice. Continue heating about 2 minutes until hot.

Green beans topped with a tangy mustard sauce. What an accompaniment for your next pork roast!

MUSTARDY BEANS

½ cup water
½ teaspoon salt
2 cups (1-lb. can) cut green beans*
2 tablespoons plain yogurt
¼ teaspoon instant minced onion
½ teaspoon prepared mustard
¼ teaspoon Worcestershire sauce

        4 (½ cup) SERVINGS
        20 Calories Each

In medium saucepan, bring water and salt to a boil. Add beans. Reduce heat; simmer 8 to 10 minutes until tender. Drain. Combine remaining ingredients; mix well. Pour sauce over beans; toss lightly. Serve hot.

Tip: *If desired, 1¾ cups (10-oz. pkg.) frozen green beans can be used for the canned beans.

BRUSSELS SPROUTS

Amount to purchase for 4 servings:
1 lb., (4 cups)

Peak season: Fall to early spring.

Look for: The miniature heads of cabbage should be firm, compact and bright green in color. Yellow heads are inferior in quality.

Basic preparation: Remove wilted outer leaves. Wash thoroughly. Cut off stems.

Storage: Place in airtight container and refrigerate for 1 to 2 days.

Cooking time and method: Cook in small amount of water, loosely covered.
Boil: 10 to 20 minutes.
Steam: 10 to 20 minutes.
Pressure cook: 1 to 2 minutes.

Source of vitamin C.

Seasonings, Spices and Herbs: Lemon juice, garlic, pepper, caraway, parsley, tarragon, thyme, bay leaf.

Sweet-sour Brussels sprouts topped with crisp bacon. Great fix-up for sprouts in only 30 minutes.

GERMAN SPROUTS

1¾ cups (10-oz. pkg.) frozen Brussels sprouts
2 slices bacon
2 tablespoons sugar
1 teaspoon salt
2 tablespoons vinegar
1 tablespoon chopped pimiento, if desired
½ cup cold water
1½ teaspoons cornstarch

4 (½ cup) SERVINGS
87 Calories Each

Cook Brussels sprouts as directed on package; drain well. In same saucepan, fry bacon until crisp; drain bacon on paper towel, reserving 1 teaspoon drippings. To reserved bacon drippings, add sugar, salt, vinegar, pimiento and ¼ cup of the water. Combine cornstarch with remaining ¼ cup water; add to vinegar mixture in saucepan. Cook over medium heat, stirring constantly, until thickened and clear. Add Brussels sprouts; heat through. Sprinkle with crisp, crumbled bacon.

CARROTS AND SPROUTS

¼ cup water
¼ cup chopped green onion
1 teaspoon sugar
¼ teaspoon salt
¼ teaspoon ground thyme
1¾ cups (10-oz. pkg.) frozen Brussels sprouts
½ cup (1 med.) carrot slices

4 (½ cup) SERVINGS
42 Calories Each

In medium saucepan, bring water, sugar, salt, thyme and onion to a boil. Add Brussels sprouts and carrot slices; simmer, covered, 5 to 8 minutes until tender. Drain; serve hot.

SUNNY SPROUTS

1¾ cups (10-oz. pkg.) frozen Brussels sprouts
½ cup (1 med. stalk) sliced celery
½ cup (1 med.) thinly sliced carrot
½ teaspoon salt
½ teaspoon sugar
½ cup water
1 teaspoon butter or margarine, melted
1 teaspoon prepared mustard
¼ teaspoon salt
Dash ground pepper or cayenne pepper

6 (½ cup) SERVINGS
32 Calories Each

In small saucepan, combine Brussels sprouts, celery, carrot, salt, sugar and water; bring to boil and cook, covered, for about 8 minutes until tender. Drain well. Combine remaining ingredients. Add to vegetables; toss lightly. Serve immediately.

Tip: If desired, 2 cups (1 lb.) fresh Brussels sprouts may be used for the frozen.

Don't overcook vegetables — they get soggy and lose many important nutrients.

CABBAGE

Amount to purchase for 4 servings:
I lb., (I small head)

Peak season: All year, (green); late summer, (red).

Look for: Heads should be firm and heavy. Leaves should be light in color and crisp.

Basic preparation: Remove wilted outer leaves. Cut into wedges or shred.

Storage: Place in crisper or in airtight container in lower part of refrigerator for I to 2 weeks.

Cooking time and method: Cook only in the water that clings to leaves, tightly covered. When cooking red cabbage, add a little lemon juice or vinegar to water to retain red color.
Boil quartered: I0 to I5 minutes.
Boil shredded: 3 to I0 minutes.
Steam quartered: I5 minutes.
Steam shredded: 8 to I2 minutes.
Pressure cook quartered: 2 to 3 minutes.
Pressure cook shredded: ½ to I minute.

Source of vitamin C.

Seasonings, Spices and Herbs: Tabasco sauce, garlic, pepper, mustard, caraway, ground cloves, parsley, tarragon, thyme, bay leaf, dill.

Flavorful hot slaw in only 30 minutes. Sliced radishes and celery add a nice crunch; bacon adds a great flavor.

PENNSYLVANIA HOT SLAW

  2 slices bacon
  I tablespoon brown sugar
  I tablespoon chopped green onion
    or chopped chives
  I teaspoon salt
¼ cup vinegar
  3 cups (½ med. head) thinly sliced cabbage
¼ cup thinly sliced radishes
¼ cup (I small stalk) thinly sliced celery

4 (½ cup) SERVINGS
69 Calories Each

In medium fry pan, fry bacon until crisp; drain bacon on paper towel, reserving I teaspoon drippings. To reserved bacon drippings, add brown sugar, green onion, salt and vinegar; stir until smooth. Add crumbled bacon and remaining ingredients; toss lightly. Heat through. Serve immediately. If desired, garnish with parsley.

CHEESY CABBAGE

¼ cup water
½ teaspoon salt
¼ teaspoon instant minced onion
  4 cups (I small head) shredded cabbage
¼ cup shredded Cheddar cheese

4 (½ cup) SERVINGS
52 Calories Each

In large saucepan, bring water, salt and onion to a boil. Add cabbage; simmer, covered, for 5 to 7 minutes until tender. Drain; sprinkle with cheese; stir lightly. Serve hot.

Sweet and sour red cabbage with chopped green apples. The longer it simmers, the better the flavor.

SWEET 'N SOUR RED CABBAGE

  6 cups (I med. head) shredded red cabbage
I½ cups (2 med.) chopped tart green apples
½ cup water
¼ cup vinegar
¼ cup firmly packed brown sugar
  I teaspoon salt
  Dash pepper

8 (½ cup) SERVINGS
6I Calories Each

In medium saucepan, combine all ingredients. Cover and simmer about I hour.

Tips: For a more sour cabbage, 2 tablespoons additional vinegar can be added.

For a different flavor, ½ teaspoon caraway seed can be added.

CAULIFLOWER

Amount to purchase for 4 servings:
I large head, (2 to 3½ lbs.)

Peak season: All year.

Look for: Head should be clean, heavy and compact. The color should be white to creamy white; outer leaves should be fresh and crisp.

Basic preparation: Remove outer leaves. Cut off tough part of stems. Wash thoroughly. Leave whole or separate into flowerettes.

Storage: Place in refrigerator in airtight container for 2 to 3 days.

Cooking time and method: Cook in enough water to cover, loosely covered.
Boil whole: I5 to 20 minutes.
Boil flowerettes: 8 to I2 minutes.
Steam whole: 25 to 30 minutes.

Steam flowerettes: 10 to 15 minutes.
Pressure cook whole: 10 minutes.
Pressure cook flowerettes: 1½ to 2 minutes.

Source of vitamin C.

Seasonings, Spices and Herbs: Tabasco sauce, curry powder, mustard, nutmeg, celery seed, poppy seed.

TANGY CAULIFLOWER

   2 cups water
½ teaspoon salt
   1 head fresh cauliflower*
½ cup plain yogurt
   1 teaspoon instant minced onion
   1 to 2 teaspoons prepared mustard
½ teaspoon Worcestershire sauce

6 (½ cup) SERVINGS
27 Calories Each

In large saucepan, bring water and salt to a boil; add cauliflower. Reduce heat; simmer 15 to 20 minutes until tender. Drain. Combine yogurt, onion, mustard and Worcestershire sauce; mix well. Spread yogurt mixture over cauliflower. Cover; allow to stand until cauliflower has heated sauce. Serve hot.

Tip: *If desired, 1½ cups (10-oz. pkg.) frozen cauliflower can be used for the whole fresh. Cook as directed on package; drain and use half of yogurt mixture.

Cauliflower cooked in bouillon to give a hint of chicken flavor. Try serving it with oven fried chicken.

COUNTRY CAULIFLOWER

½ cup water*
½ teaspoon salt
   1 chicken bouillon cube or 1 teaspoon
      instant bouillon
1½ cups (10-oz. pkg.) frozen cauli-
      flowerettes**

3 (½ cup) SERVINGS
11 Calories Each

In small saucepan, combine water, salt and bouillon; bring to a boil. Add frozen cauliflowerettes; bring to a boil. Reduce heat; simmer 5 to 7 minutes until tender. Drain. If desired, garnish with chopped parsley.

Tips: *½ cup chicken broth can be used for the water and chicken bouillon.

**1¼ cups (¼ head) fresh cauliflower, separated into pieces, can be used for the frozen. Simmer 10 to 15 minutes until tender.

Add zip to your corn on the cob. Just baste with dry onion soup mixed with water and salt. Yum! Try on barbecue grill, too!

ONION CORN ON THE COB

   1 envelope (1¼-oz. pkg.) onion soup mix
½ cup water
½ teaspoon salt
   8 ears corn

OVEN 425°   8 SERVINGS
117 Calories Each

In small mixing bowl, combine onion soup mix, water and salt; mix well. Place each ear on piece of foil. Spread each ear of corn with 1 tablespoon onion soup mixture. Wrap ears tightly in foil. Bake at 425° for 30 to 35 minutes until tender.

Tip: Wrapped ears of corn can be placed on grill over hot coals. Cook as directed.

CORN

Amount to purchase for 4 servings:
1 to 2 ears per person
(2 ears = 1 cup kernels)

Peak season: Summer.

Look for: Green husks with cobs filled with plump, juicy kernels.

Basic preparation: Remove husk and silk; trim ends. Wash thoroughly. Leave whole or cut kernels from cob with sharp knife. For cream-style corn, cut kernels only halfway to cob; then scrape cob with dull edge of knife.

Storage: Store unhusked and uncovered in refrigerator for 1 to 2 days.

Cooking time and method: Cook kernels in small amount of water, tightly covered. Cook on cob covered with water, tightly covered.
Boil on cob: 3 to 5 minutes.
Boil kernels: 5 to 8 minutes.
Steam on cob: 10 to 15 minutes.
Steam kernels: 12 to 15 minutes.
Pressure cook on cob: ½ to 1 minute.
Pressure cook kernels: ½ to 1 minute.
Bake on cob: 20 to 25 minutes.

Seasonings, Spices and Herbs: Cayenne, curry powder, chili powder, pepper, parsley, bay leaf, chives, basil.

ORANGEY CARROTS

   3 cups (6 med.) carrots, cut into 2-inch
      pieces
¼ teaspoon salt
¼ teaspoon paprika
½ cup orange juice
   2 tablespoons chopped onion or 1 teaspoon
      instant minced onion

OVEN 350°   6 (½ cup) SERVINGS
                  37 Calories Each

In ungreased 1½ to 2-quart casserole or baking dish, combine all ingredients. Stir to mix well. Bake, covered, at 350° for 1 hour until tender. Serve with sauce.

Tip: To make in saucepan, combine all ingredients. Simmer, stirring occasionally, for 30 minutes until heated and flavors have blended.

MOCK CARROTS IN CREME'

   2 cups (4 med.) sliced carrots
½ cup water
  1 teaspoon salt
   Dash pepper, if desired
  1 teaspoon parsley flakes
  2 tablespoons plain yogurt

                 4 (½ cup) SERVINGS
                 32 Calories Each

In medium saucepan, bring carrots, water and salt to a boil. Simmer, covered, for 10 to 12 minutes until tender. Drain well. Add pepper, parsley and yogurt; stir to mix well. Serve hot.

CARROTS OLE'

   4 strips bacon, crumbled
½ cup water
  1 teaspoon salt
  2 cups (4 med.) shredded carrots
  2 tablespoons chopped chives or green
     onion, if desired

                 4 (½ cup) SERVINGS
                 79 Calories Each

Fry bacon until crisp; drain thoroughly on paper towel. In small saucepan, bring water and salt to a boil. Add carrots, chives and bacon. Simmer, covered, 10 to 12 minutes until tender. Drain and serve.

Tips: Leftover carrots can be chilled and served as a salad. Or, Carrots Olé can be chilled, uncooked, and served crisp.

If desired, 2 tablespoons bacon-flavored bits can be used for the bacon.

CARROTS

Amount to purchase for 4 servings:
1 lb., (about 8 medium)

Peak season: All year.

Look for: Carrots should be firm, well shaped, smooth and bright golden in color. Tops should be green and fresh looking. The tops may be cut off. Young carrots have extra long rootlets.

Basic preparation: Scrape or peel with vegetable peeler to remove thin layer of skin. Cut off tops and tips. Tops may be added to tossed salads. Leave whole, slice, chop or cut into strips.

Storage: Rinse carrots after removing tops. Place moist carrots in airtight container in refrigerator for 1 to 2 weeks. Keep carrots moist during storage.

Cooking time and method: Cook in small amount of water, tightly covered.
Boil whole: 20 to 25 minutes.
Boil sliced: 15 to 20 minutes.
Steam whole: 25 to 30 minutes.
Steam sliced: 20 to 25 minutes.
Pressure cook whole: 3 to 4 minutes.
Pressure cook sliced: 1½ to 2 minutes.
Bake whole: 35 to 40 minutes.
Bake sliced: 30 to 35 minutes.

Source of vitamin A.

Seasonings, Spices and Herbs: ginger, mace, pepper, allspice, anise seed, caraway, ground cloves, parsley, peppermint, spearmint, thyme, bay leaf, dill.

Store unopened canned vegetables in a cool, dry place.

Purchase only frozen vegetables properly stored in freezer display. Avoid vegetables that are not firmly frozen.

Remove tops from fresh beets, carrots and radishes for longer storage.

EGGPLANT

Amount to purchase for 4 servings:
I medium (I½ lbs.)

Peak season: Summer.

Look for: Choose firm, heavy eggplants, free of blemishes. Skin should be a clear, dark purple glossy color. Dull-skinned eggplant is usually overripe and tough.

Basic preparation: Wash and peel if skin is tough. Cut off stem. Slice, cube or leave whole. Dip into lemon juice to prevent darkening.

Storage: Keep at cool room temperature (about 50°F.) in airtight container for 3 to 4 days.

Cooking time and method: Cook in small amount of water, covered tightly.
Boil: 20 to 25 minutes.
Steam: 30 minutes.

Seasonings, Spices and Herbs: Tomato sauce, garlic, pepper, peppercorns, curry powder, parsley, sage, allspice, basil, oregano.

MUSHROOMS

Amount to purchase for 4 servings:
I lb. (2 pts.)

Peak season: All year.

Look for: Dry, firm mushrooms. Small brown spots or slightly opened caps do not mean inferior quality but only maturity.

Basic preparation: Wash carefully but do not peel. Cut off tips of stems. Leave whole or slice lengthwise. Mushrooms do not need to be cooked if used in salads or marinated.

Storage: Fresh mushrooms should be kept moist by placing on a tray or in an airtight container with a moist towel on top. Moisten towel daily. Store in refrigerator I to 2 days.

Cooking time and method: Sauté in melted butter until golden brown.

Seasonings, Spices and Herbs: Marjoram, rosemary, tarragon, oregano.

This dish will remind you of fried eggplant, but it has fewer calories. You'll like the crunchy texture.

BROILED EGGPLANT

   ¼ **cup dry bread crumbs or corn flake crumbs**
   2 **tablespoons grated Parmesan cheese**
I½ **teaspoons salt**
   Dash garlic salt
   8 **slices (I med.) peeled eggplant**
   I **egg, slightly beaten**

4 SERVINGS
73 Calories Each

Combine bread crumbs, cheese, salt and garlic salt. Dip eggplant slices in egg, then coat with crumb mixture. Place in shallow baking pan. Broil 5 to 7 inches from heat for 3 to 5 minutes; turn slices over and continue broiling for 3 to 5 minutes until tender. Serve hot.

Okra cooked with tomatoes and corn. A tasty combination of vegetables that makes a real partner with chicken.

PLANTATION OKRA

I½ **cups (10-oz. pkg.) frozen okra**
   2 **cups (I-lb. can) undrained tomatoes***
   I **cup (7-oz. can) corn with red and green pepper**
   ½ **cup (I med.) chopped onion or 2 tablespoons instant minced onion**
   ½ **cup (I stalk) sliced celery**
I½ **teaspoons salt**
   Dash pepper

6 (½ cup) SERVINGS
63 Calories Each

In large saucepan, combine all ingredients. Simmer, covered, for 10 to 15 minutes until tender. Drain; serve hot.

Tip: *If desired, 2 fresh tomatoes, cut into pieces, can be used for the canned tomatoes.

OKRA

Amount to purchase for 4 servings:
1 lb.

Peak season: Summer and fall.

Look for: Pods should be bright green, crisp and free from blemishes. Small to medium pods are best.

Basic preparation: Wash thoroughly. Cut off stem. Leave whole or slice.

Storage: Place in crisper of refrigerator or wrap in airtight container; store for 2 to 3 days. Keep moist during storage.

Cooking time and method: Cook in small amount of water, loosely covered.
Boil: 20 to 25 minutes.
Steam: 25 to 30 minutes.
Pressure cook: 3 to 4 minutes.

Seasonings, Spices and Herbs: Lemon juice, tomato sauce, oregano, pepper, paprika.

PEAS WITH MUSHROOMS AND ONION

   1½ cups (10-oz. pkg.) frozen peas
   ½ cup (4-oz. can) drained mushroom
       stems and pieces
   ¼ cup (½ small) chopped onion
    2 teaspoons butter or margarine
   ¼ teaspoon salt
       Dash pepper
       Dash ground allspice

4 (½ cup) SERVINGS
80 Calories Each

Cook peas as directed on package; drain well. In small saucepan, sauté mushrooms and onion in butter until tender. Add remaining ingredients. Serve immediately.

Tip: If desired, 2 cups (1-lb. can) drained peas can be used for the frozen peas.

PEAS

Amount to purchase for 4 servings:
2 lbs. (2 cups shelled)

Peak season: Early summer.

Look for: Pods should be bright green, plump and free of blemishes.

Basic preparation: Shell peas by removing from pods. Wash thoroughly.

Storage: Store, uncovered, in pods in refrigerator for 1 to 2 days.

Cooking time and method: Cook in small amount of water, loosely covered.
Boil: 8 to 20 minutes.
Steam: 10 to 20 minutes.
Pressure cook: 1 minute.

Source of vitamins A & C.

Seasonings, Spices and Herbs: Tabasco sauce, soy sauce, Worcestershire sauce, garlic, nutmeg, pepper, caraway, ground cloves, peppermint, rosemary, sage, savory, spearmint, basil, marjoram, mint.

PEA MEDLEY

   ½ cup (1 med.) chopped onion
   ¼ cup (1 small stalk) finely chopped celery
    1 tablespoon butter or margarine
   1½ cups (10-oz. pkg.) frozen peas
   ¾ teaspoon salt
   ¼ teaspoon pepper
   ⅛ teaspoon powdered marjoram
   ¼ cup water

4 (½ cup) SERVINGS
85 Calories Each

In small saucepan, sauté onion and celery in butter in saucepan until tender. Add peas, salt, pepper, marjoram and water. Cover tightly; cook 5 to 7 minutes just until peas are tender. Drain and serve.

Potatoes that taste like they were cooked with a pot roast. A quick, low calorie way to fix potatoes that will become a family favorite.

HEARTY POTATOES

   ½ cup water
   ½ teaspoon salt
   ½ teaspoon instant minced onion
    1 cube beef bouillon or 1 teaspoon instant
       bouillon
    2 cups (3 med.) sliced or quartered potatoes

4 (½ cup) SERVINGS
66 Calories Each

In large saucepan, bring water, salt, onion and beef bouillon to a boil. Add sliced potatoes; simmer, covered, 10 to 12 minutes for slices, 15 to 20 minutes for quarters, just until tender. Serve hot with liquid.

Tip: Other types of bouillon (chicken, onion, vegetable) can be used for the beef.

POTATOES

Amount to purchase for 4 servings:
2 lbs. (4 medium)

Peak season: All year.

Look for: Potatoes should be firm and well-shaped. Soft spots indicate spoilage and inferior quality.

Basic preparation: Scrub with vegetable brush or plastic scouring pad. Peel or leave skins on. Leave whole or cut in pieces, cubes or slices. Leave sweet potatoes in skin to boil or bake.

Storage: White potatoes should be kept in cool dry place for several months. Sweet potatoes should be kept at cool room temperature for several weeks. Too cool temperatures may cause chilling injury.

Cooking time and method:

White—

Boil whole: 25 to 35 minutes.
Boil quartered: 20 to 25 minutes.
Steam whole: 30 to 40 minutes.
Steam quartered: 20 to 25 minutes.
Pressure cook whole: 8 to 11 minutes.
Pressure cook quartered: 3 to 5 minutes.
Bake whole: 45 to 60 minutes at 400° F.

Sweet—

Boil whole: 25 to 30 minutes.
Steam whole: 30 to 35 minutes.
Pressure cook whole: 5 to 8 minutes.
Bake whole: 30 to 45 minutes at 400° F.

White potatoes—source of vitamin C.

Sweet potatoes—source of vitamin A.

Seasonings, Spices and Herbs: Tabasco sauce, barbecue sauce, chili sauce, garlic, curry powder, ginger, mace, mustard, nutmeg, paprika, caraway, chili powder, parsley, thyme, bay leaf, chives.

LOW CALORIE MASHED POTATOES

1 cup water
1 teaspoon salt
4 cups chopped peeled potatoes
⅓ cup skim milk
Dash pepper, if desired

4 (½ cup) SERVINGS
137 Calories Each

In large saucepan, bring water and salt to a boil. Add potatoes; simmer, covered for 10 to 12 minutes, until tender. Drain water. Add milk and pepper; mash until smooth. Serve hot.

PARSLIED POTATOES

2 cups water
1 teaspoon salt
4 cups (4 med.) quartered peeled potatoes
2 tablespoons chopped parsley or 1 teaspoon parsley flakes
½ teaspoon salt

8 (½ cup) SERVINGS
66 Calories Each

In large saucepan, bring water and 1 teaspoon salt to a boil. Add potatoes; cook, covered, over medium heat for 15 to 20 minutes until tender. Drain. Add parsley and ½ teaspoon salt; stir lightly to coat potatoes. Serve hot.

Tip: For Dilly Potatoes, use ⅛ teaspoon dill weed for the parsley.

EASY MASHED POTATOES

1½ cups water
½ teaspoon salt
½ cup skim milk
1½ cups Pillsbury Hungry Jack Potato Flakes

4 (½ cup) SERVINGS
47 Calories Each

In small saucepan, bring water and salt to a boil. Remove from heat; add milk. Add potato flakes all at one time. Stir several times with fork, just to moisten. Let stand several minutes. Serve hot.

SPINACH:

Amount to purchase for 4 servings:
1 lb. (about 4 cups)

Peak season: All year.

Look for: Leaves should be fresh, tender and bright green in color. Yellowing leaves are inferior in quality.

Basic preparation: Wash with cold water. Remove wilted leaves and tough stems or ribs.

Storage: Place washed and drained leaves in crisper of refrigerator for 2 to 3 days.

Cooking time and method: Cook in the water which clings to leaves after washing, tightly covered.

Boil: 3 to 10 minutes.
Steam: 3 to 10 minutes.
Pressure cook: 1 to 2 minutes.

Source of vitamins A & C.

Seasonings, Spices and Herbs: Herb or wine vinegar, mace, nutmeg, paprika, pepper, ground cloves, rosemary, tarragon, marjoram, mint.

SNAPPLE SPINACH

½ **cup water**
¼ **teaspoon salt**
 8 **cups chopped fresh spinach***
½ **cup (I med.) grated carrot**
½ **cup (I small) chopped apple**

4 (½ cup) SERVINGS
43 Calories Each

In large saucepan, bring water and salt to a boil. Add spinach, carrot and apple; simmer, covered, for 3 to 5 minutes until tender. Drain. Serve hot.

Tip: *If desired, 2 cups (I-lb. can) undrained spinach can be used for the fresh. Omit water; cook in canned liquid. Or, 1½ cups (10-oz. pkg.) frozen spinach can be used, preparing as directed on package and adding carrot and apple with spinach.

SPINACH IN TOMATOES

 I **cup (8-oz. can) undrained tomatoes**
 2 **teaspoons finely chopped onion or**
 ½ **teaspoon instant minced onion**
 I **teaspoon salt**
 I **teaspoon parsley flakes, if desired**
 8 **cups fresh spinach***

6 (½ cup) SERVINGS
19 Calories Each

In large saucepan, bring tomatoes, onion, salt and parsley flakes to a boil. Add spinach; simmer, covered, 3 to 5 minutes until tender. Drain extra liquid; serve hot.

Tip: *If desired, 2 cups (I-lb. can) well-drained spinach or 1½ cups (10-oz. pkg.) frozen spinach can be used for the fresh. Add to tomato mixture and heat through or cook until tender.

SESAME SPINACH

 I **tablespoon sesame seeds**
 I **tablespoon soy sauce**
1½ **cups (10-oz. pkg.) frozen spinach**

3 (½ cup) SERVINGS
43 Calories Each

In fry pan on medium heat, brown sesame seeds. Reduce heat; add soy sauce and spinach. Cover; simmer 7 to 10 minutes until tender.

Tip: For 6 servings, double all ingredients.

To crisp vegetable greens such as cabbage or spinach, place in airtight container with cold, wet towel over the vegetable. Chill in refrigerator at least one hour.

SPINACH ROYALE

1¾ **cups (10-oz. pkg.) frozen spinach**
 ½ **cup (4-oz. can) drained and sliced mushrooms**
 2 **teaspoons finely chopped onion or**
 ½ **teaspoon instant minced onion**
 Dash pepper
 Dash garlic salt
 ¼ **cup hot water**
 ¼ **teaspoon salt**
 I **tablespoon plain yogurt**

4 (½ cup) SERVINGS
30 Calories Each

Prepare spinach as directed on package, adding mushrooms, onion, pepper and garlic salt with spinach; drain thoroughly. Add yogurt; mix lightly. Serve hot.

Tip: Canned spinach can be used for the frozen. Omit water and salt. Just heat in canned liquid, along with mushrooms, onion, pepper and garlic salt; drain and stir in yogurt.

This quick stew will remind you of autumn. Serve it with beef for a tasty combination.

HARVEST STEW

 2 **tomatoes, quartered***
 I **cup (I med.) sliced zucchini**
 I **cup (8-oz. can) cut green beans**
 I **cup (8-oz. can) corn**
 I **cup (2 med. stalks) sliced celery, reserve tops**
 I **teaspoon salt**
 I **teaspoon instant minced onion or I small onion, sliced**
 Reserved celery tops

6 (½ cup) SERVINGS
50 Calories Each

In large saucepan, combine all ingredients. Bring to a boil. Reduce heat; simmer, covered, 10 to 12 minutes until tender. Drain; remove celery tops. Serve hot.

Tips: If desired, use I cup (8-oz. can) undrained tomatoes for the fresh; omit water.

A 10-oz. package frozen zucchini can be used for the fresh.

VEGETABLE STUFFED TOMATOES

1¾ cup (10-oz. pkg.) frozen mixed vegetables*
4 fresh tomatoes

4 SERVINGS
97 Calories Each

Cook frozen vegetables as directed on package; drain. Cut off tops of tomatoes and hollow out centers. Spoon ½ cup of hot vegetables into each tomato. Serve hot or chill and serve with salad dressing.

Tips: *Canned or frozen peas and carrots can be used for the mixed vegetables. To use canned vegetables, just heat, drain and spoon into tomato cups.

Tomatoes can be stuffed ahead of time. Heat at 350° for 10 minutes before serving.

SEASONED VEGETABLES

1¾ cups (10-oz. pkg.) frozen peas and carrots*
¼ teaspoon Italian or French salad dressing mix**

4 (½ cup) SERVINGS
47 Calories Each

Cook peas and carrots as directed on package. Drain; sprinkle salad dressing mix over vegetables. Allow to stand, covered, several minutes until flavors blend. Serve hot.

Tips: *Canned peas and carrots can be used for the frozen. Heat in liquids from can. Drain; add salad dressing mix.

**Any of the dry salad dressing mixes can be used for seasoning. We particularly like garlic cheese and Italian.

Leftovers? Toss them in with your lettuce salad tomorrow night.

Other vegetables can be used for the peas and carrots; however, their calorie counts will vary accordingly.

Unripe tomatoes can be ripened by storing at room temperature until ripe, then refrigerate. Do not store in direct sunlight, as uneven ripening is the result.

Cook frozen vegetables in the oven at the same temperature as your meat dish. What a convenience to be able to prepare your entire meal in the oven!

OVEN BAKED FROZEN VEGETABLES

1½ to 2 cups (9 to 10-oz. pkg.) frozen vegetables
2 tablespoons water
¼ teaspoon salt

OVEN 350°   4 SERVINGS
Calories Vary According To Vegetable

Place frozen vegetables in ungreased 1 to 1½-quart casserole or baking dish. Top with water and salt. Bake, covered, according to time table below until tender.

VEGETABLE	MINUTES
Cut asparagus	50 to 60
Asparagus spears	50 to 60
Chopped broccoli	40 to 50
Broccoli spears	35 to 45
Cauliflower	45 to 55
Corn	40 to 50
Beans	
Green	
Cut	50 to 60
French-style	50 to 60
Italian	50 to 60
Whole	50 to 60
Lima	
Baby	50 to 60
Fordhook	40 to 50
Wax	50 to 60
Mixed vegetables	50 to 60
Peas	40 to 50
Peas and carrots	50 to 60
Spinach leaves	40 to 50
Chopped spinach	40 to 50
Succotash	50 to 60

Tips: To bake at 325°, increase time about 10 minutes.

To bake at 375°, decrease time about 10 minutes.

SQUASH

Summer varieties: Zucchini, pattypan, crookneck yellow.

Amount to purchase for 4 servings:
1½ lbs.

Peak season: Summer.

Look for: Summer varieties should be heavy with smooth, bright colored skin. Skin will be soft enough to puncture easily with fingernail.

Basic preparation: Wash but do not peel. Remove stem, blossom end, seeds and fibers. Leave whole, slice or chop.

Storage: Place in crisper of refrigerator for several days.

Cooking time and method: Cook in small amount of water, tightly covered.
Boil 10 to 20 minutes.
Steam: 15 to 20 minutes.
Pressure cook: 1½ to 2 minutes.

Seasonings, Spices and Herbs: Ginger, mace, nutmeg, pepper, allspice, ground cloves, parsley, savory, spearmint, bay leaf.

Winter varieties: Banana, butternut, hubbard, acorn.

Amount to purchase for 4 servings:
1½ lbs.

Peak season: Winter

Look for: All winter varieties should be heavy and bright colored. Rind should be hard and thick.

Basic preparation: Acorn — Wash; do not peel. Cut in half and remove seeds.
Hubbard — Peel if skin is tough. Remove seeds and fibers. Cut into serving pieces.
Banana — Wash; do not peel. Cut into serving pieces.
Butternut — Wash; cut into serving pieces and remove seeds.

Storage: Whole squash can be stored in cool dry place for several months. Cut pieces can be placed in airtight container in crisper for 1 to 2 days.

Cooking time and method: Cook in small amount of water, tightly covered.
Boil acorn: 15 to 20 minutes.
Steam acorn: 25 to 30 minutes.
Pressure cook acorn: 6 to 12 minutes.
Bake acorn: 40 to 50 minutes at 400°.
Boil hubbard: 15 to 20 minutes.
Steam hubbard: 25 to 30 minutes.
Pressure cook hubbard: 6 to 12 minutes.
Bake hubbard: 45 to 50 minutes at 400°.

Boil banana: 15 to 20 minutes.
Steam banana: 25 to 30 minutes.
Pressure cook banana: 6 to 12 minutes.
Bake banana: 25 to 30 minutes at 400°.
Boil butternut: 20 to 25 minutes.
Steam butternut: 30 to 35 minutes.
Bake butternut: 50 to 60 minutes at 400°.

Source of vitamin A.

Slices of Zucchini squash in an Italian-flavored sauce. Try the tip with mushrooms, too.

ZUCCHINI ITALIAN

½ cup water
½ teaspoon salt
  Dash pepper
  Dash oregano or Italian seasoning
  Dash garlic powder, if desired
3 cups (3 med.) sliced zucchini
¼ cup tomato paste

4 (½ cup) SERVINGS
33 Calories Each

In medium saucepan, bring water, salt, pepper, oregano, and garlic powder to a boil. Add zucchini. Reduce heat; cover and simmer 5 to 7 minutes until tender. Drain. Stir in tomato paste. Reheat over very low heat until hot.

Tip: If desired, add ½ cup (4-oz. can) drained small mushrooms or mushroom pieces with the zucchini.

Two popular types of squash combine to make this dish. Subtle seasoning gives them a flair. Try the tip for Dilly Squash, too!

SUMMER SQUASH DUO

½ cup water
½ teaspoon salt
½ teaspoon instant minced onion
⅛ teaspoon ground thyme*
2 cups (2 med.) sliced summer squash
2 cups (2 med.) sliced zucchini

6 (½ cup) SERVINGS
26 Calories Each

In medium saucepan, combine water, salt, onion and thyme. Bring to a boil. Add summer squash and zucchini; reduce heat and simmer, covered, for 5 to 8 minutes until tender. Drain liquid; serve hot.

Tip: *For Dilly Squash, ⅛ teaspoon dill weed can be used for the thyme.

SQUASH 'N PEPPERS

½ **cup water**
½ **teaspoon sugar**
¼ **teaspoon salt**
¼ **teaspoon leaf oregano or Italian seasoning**
¼ **teaspoon leaf basil**
2 **cups (2 med.) sliced summer squash**
1 **green pepper, seeded and sliced, if desired**
2 **cups (2 med.) quartered tomatoes**
1 **teaspoon wine vinegar or cider vinegar**

6 (½ cup) SERVINGS
24 Calories Each

In large saucepan, bring water, sugar, salt, oregano and basil to a boil. Add squash and pepper; simmer, covered, 5 minutes. Add tomatoes and vinegar, continue simmering 2 to 3 minutes until squash is tender. Drain and serve.

MEXI-SQUASH

¼ **cup water**
1 **tablespoon chopped pimiento**
½ **teaspoon salt**
½ **teaspoon parsley flakes**
2 **cups (2 med.) sliced summer squash**

3 (½ cup) SERVINGS
27 Calories Each

In medium saucepan, combine all ingredients except squash. Bring to a boil. Add squash; reduce heat. Simmer, covered, for 5 to 8 minutes until tender. Drain. Serve hot.

TOMATOES

Amount to purchase for 4 servings:
1½ lbs. (4 medium)

Peak season: Available all year, peak in summer.

Look for: Choose somewhat firm, bright red colored tomatoes, free of deep blemishes. Avoid deep red colored ones as they may be overripe.

Basic preparation: Wash; peel if desired. Cut out stem. Leave whole, quarter or slice.

Storage: Store in cool place or in refrigerator.

Cooking time and method: Cook in no water, just the natural tomato juices, tightly covered. Boil: 7 to 15 minutes.
Steam: ½ to 1 minute.
Pressure cook: ½ to 1 minute.

Source of vitamin C.

Seasonings, Spices and Herbs: Garlic, herb or wine vinegar, curry powder, pepper, allspice, sage, thyme, basil, bay leaf, oregano.

A great new way to serve cherry tomatoes. Sauté, then add seasoning. The color in this dish will add snazz to your meal.

CHERRY FRIES

1 **teaspoon butter or margarine**
2 **cups (8 oz. or 1 pt.) cherry tomatoes, washed and stemmed**
¼ **teaspoon salt**
⅛ **to ¼ teaspoon leaf basil or leaf rosemary, if desired**
Dash pepper

4 (½ cup) SERVINGS
31 Calories Each

In fry pan, melt butter. Add tomatoes, salt, basil and pepper; mix well. Cook, uncovered, over medium heat, stirring occasionally, about 5 minutes until tender. Serve hot.

PARSLIED TOMATOES

2 **cups (3 med.) sliced tomatoes**
1 **cup (2 stalks) sliced celery, if desired**
¼ **cup chopped fresh parsley or 1 tablespoon parsley flakes**
½ **cup wine vinegar or cider vinegar**
½ **teaspoon salt**
¼ **teaspoon Italian seasoning or crushed oregano, if desired**

6 SERVINGS
24 Calories Each

Combine all ingredients; toss lightly. Chill, covered, at least 2 hours. Drain extra liquid. (This can be used as a dressing for other salads.) Serve on lettuce leaves.

CHEESE BROILED TOMATO

2 **fresh whole tomatoes**
1 **tablespoon chopped green onion or chives**
1 **teaspoon parsley flakes**
½ **teaspoon salt**
1 **tablespoon grated Parmesan cheese**

4 (½ cup) SERVINGS
30 Calories Each

Cut tomatoes in half. Place cut-side up in baking pan. Sprinkle onion, parsley, salt and cheese evenly over halves. Broil 3 to 4 inches from heat for 5 minutes until heated through and cheese in golden brown. Serve immediately.

Desserts

BAKED CUSTARD

3 eggs
½ cup sugar
¼ teaspoon salt
I teaspoon vanilla extract
2½ cups skim milk
Dash nutmeg

OVEN 350°   6 (½ cup) SERVINGS
                             140 Calories Each

In medium mixing bowl, combine eggs, sugar, salt and vanilla extract; add milk. Pour into six custard cups. Sprinkle with nutmeg. Place cups in a 13x9-inch pan filled I-inch deep with hot water. Bake at 350° for 35 to 40 minutes, until a knife inserted in center comes out clean. Serve warm or chilled.

CREAM PUFFS

½ cup water
¼ cup cooking oil
½ cup flour
¼ teaspoon salt
2 eggs
I½ cups whipped topping
I to 2 teaspoons extract*
2 tablespoons powdered sugar

OVEN 425°   6 SERVINGS
                             187 Calories Each

In medium saucepan, heat water and oil just to boiling. Add flour and salt all at once. Stir hard until flour clumps into ball in center of pan. Let stand 5 minutes. Add I egg at a time, beating until blended after each egg. Place by tablespoons on ungreased cookie sheet. Bake at 425° for 20 minutes until all beads of moisture have disappeared. Cool. Cut tops off. Mix whipped topping with extract. Fill puffs. Replace tops. Sprinkle lightly with powdered sugar.

Tips: *Any flavor extract can be used. We particularly like orange and lemon.

Creme de menthe or other flavors of liqueurs can also be used for the extract, if desired.

To make ahead, prepare puffs early in the day. Cover. Before serving, fill with whipped topping.

MERINGUE SHELLS

2 egg whites
⅛ teaspoon cream of tartar
I teaspoon vanilla extract
¼ teaspoon salt
⅔ cup sugar

OVEN 275°   8 SERVINGS
                             68 Calories Each

In small mixer bowl, beat egg whites with cream of tartar, vanilla extract and salt until soft peaks form. Gradually add sugar and continue beating until very stiff peaks form. Spoon meringue onto brown paper on cookie sheets, using a heaping tablespoonful for each. Make a deep well in the center of each, spreading out to make a shell 3-inches in diameter. Bake at 275° for about I hour, until crisp and very lightly browned. Cool a few minutes before removing from paper. Cool completely. Fill shells with fruit.

Tip: Meringues can be frozen or stored in a dry place in a tightly covered container. Meringues can be made into other shapes such as hearts.

Top this nutritious pan cake with fresh fruit for a positively plush breakfast, lunch or dessert idea!

GERMAN PANCAKES

4 eggs
⅔ cup flour
I tablespoon sugar
½ teaspoon salt
⅔ cup skim milk
2 tablespoons cooking oil

OVEN 400°   4 SERVINGS
                             234 Calories Each

Grease two 9-inch round pans. In medium mixing bowl, beat eggs slightly. Add remaining ingredients; mix well. Pour batter into pans. Bake at 400° for 20 minutes. Reduce heat to 350°; continue baking for 10 minutes. Slide onto plates. Serve with fruit.

Tip: To make in blender, process eggs on low speed until light yellow in color. Add remaining ingredients; process on medium speed until blended. Bake as directed.

A thin, nutritious pancake that can be filled with fruit for breakfast or dessert, or filled with meat for a lunch or supper dish.

BASIC CREPES

⅔ cup skim milk
I tablespoon cooking oil
2 eggs
½ cup flour
I teaspoon sugar
¼ teaspoon salt
I teaspoon cooking oil

SIX 7-INCH CREPES
100 Calories Each

In medium mixer bowl, combine milk, I tablespoon oil and eggs with rotary beater or mixer at low speed. Add flour, sugar and salt; continue beating until smooth. Heat I teaspoon oil in a 7-inch fry pan over medium heat until drops of water "dance". Pour ¼ cup batter into pan all at once; tilt to spread over bottom of pan. Cook, turning once, until light brown on both sides. Fill with your choice of fillings; roll up.

Tips: Use your imagination for interesting fillings. For idea starters, try:

¼ cup drained fresh or canned peaches
¼ cup fresh or frozen berries
¼ cup Creamed Tuna, page 92

For those not watching calories, top fruit-filled crepes with whipped topping or ice cream.

To make ahead, roll after cooking. Store, covered, for I or 2 days in refrigerator. Fill, reheat at 325° for 20 to 25 minutes until heated through.

For a delightful company dessert, top each fruit-filled crepe with I tablespoon liqueur. Flambé, if desired.

To make Cheese-Filled Blintzes, combine I cup (8 oz. or ½ pt.) cottage cheese, I tablespoon sugar and ¼ teaspoon cinnamon; mix well. Spoon mixture into Basic Crepes; roll. Heat at 400° for 5 minutes; or cover and refrigerate until serving time. Reheat at 325° for 20 to 25 minutes. If desired, top with whipped topping or sour cream.

TAPIOCA PUDDING

2 eggs, separated
2 cups skim milk
⅓ cup sugar
2 tablespoons quick-cooking tapioca
¼ teaspoon salt
I teaspoon vanilla extract

6 (½ cup) SERVINGS
110 Calories Each

In medium saucepan, combine egg yolks, milk, ¼ cup of the sugar, tapioca and salt. Cook over medium heat, stirring constantly, until mixture comes to a full boil. Remove from heat. Blend in vanilla extract. In large mixer bowl, beat egg whites until soft peaks form. Gradually add remaining 4 teaspoons sugar; beat until sugar dissolves. Fold in tapioca mixture gently but thoroughly. Spoon into serving dishes. Cool.

Tips: For flavor variety, sprinkle top of tapioca with ground cloves, nutmeg or cinnamon.

For Fruity Tapioca, add ½ cup drained crushed pineapple or other fruit to mixture before chilling.

Use leftover rice in this hearty and nutritious dessert. Serve cold for breakfast or lunch, too.

SWEDISH RICE PUDDING

2 eggs, beaten
1½ cups skim milk
⅓ cup sugar
½ teaspoon vanilla extract
¼ teaspoon cinnamon
⅛ teaspoon ground nutmeg
½ cup cooked rice
¼ cup raisins, if desired

OVEN 350°   6 SERVINGS
122 Calories Each

In 1½ or 2-quart casserole, combine all ingredients; mix thoroughly. Place casserole in pan filled I-inch deep with hot water. Bake at 350° for 45 to 60 minutes, until a knife inserted halfway between center and edge of dish comes out clean. Serve warm or cold.

Tips: Pudding will bake with a custard layer on top. For a more even distribution of rice and raisins, stir pudding carefully after 30 minutes of baking.

For Lemon Rice Pudding, use lemon extract for vanilla extract; add I teaspoon grated lemon peel.

Light and airy, this nutritious dessert makes an elegant ending to any meal. Time it to come out of the oven just as you're ready for dessert.

LEMONY SOUFFLÉ

I tablespoon butter or margarine
2 tablespoons flour
¼ teaspoon salt
⅔ cup sugar
½ cup water
¼ cup lemon juice
4 egg yolks, reserve whites
I tablespoon grated lemon rind
Reserved 4 egg whites

OVEN 325°   6 (I cup) SERVINGS
166 Calories Each

Melt butter in saucepan. Blend in flour and salt. Add ⅓ cup sugar, water and lemon juice. Cook over medium heat, stirring constantly, until thick. Blend a little of the hot mixture into egg yolks. Stir into remaining hot mixture; add lemon rind. Mix thoroughly. Beat reserved egg whites in large mixer bowl until soft peaks form. Gradually add ⅓ cup sugar, beating until stiff peaks form. Fold egg yolk mixture gently but thoroughly into egg whites. Pour into 1½-quart casserole. With flat side of knife or small metal spatula, trace a circle around top of soufflé about I-inch in from edge and ½-inch deep. Place in pan filled I-inch deep with hot water. Bake at 325° for 55 to 60 minutes until golden brown. Serve immediately.

MINTY FRUIT CUP

I cup seedless green grapes, halved
2 bananas, sliced
3 oranges, peeled and sectioned
½ cup orange juice
I teaspoon dry or fresh mint leaves
I cup strawberries, whole or sliced

6 (I cup) SERVINGS
114 Calories Each

Combine grapes, bananas, oranges, orange juice and mint leaves in mixing bowl. Stir carefully. Refrigerate at least 2 hours. Stir occasionally to mix fruits with juice. Just before serving, add strawberries. Spoon into serving dishes. If desired, top with fresh mint leaves.

Tip: For those not watching calories, top with a scoop of orange sherbet, if desired.

A new twist on a traditional idea, this chilled dessert is a blend of spice and pumpkin — light and fluffy.

PUMPKIN CHIFFON

I tablespoon (I envelope) unflavored gelatin
½ cup cold water
2 eggs, separated
I cup canned or cooked pumpkin
⅓ cup sugar
I teaspoon vanilla
½ teaspoon cinnamon
¼ teaspoon salt
¼ teaspoon nutmeg
⅓ cup instant nonfat dry milk
⅓ cup ice water*

8 (½ cup) SERVINGS
74 Calories Each

Chill small mixer bowl and beaters in refrigerator. In medium saucepan, soften gelatin in cold water. Heat over medium heat until gelatin dissolves. Add egg yolk, pumpkin, sugar, vanilla, cinnamon, salt and nutmeg; stir until well blended. Chill until slightly thickened but not set. In small, chilled mixer bowl, beat nonfat dry milk, ice water and egg whites at high speed until stiff peaks form. Fold into pumpkin mixture. Carefully pour into serving dishes. Chill about 2 hours until firm.

Tips: *Place a few ice cubes in water until ice cold; this is essential for proper whipping.

For those not watching calories, top serving with whipped topping. Or, pour part of mixture into an 8-inch graham cracker pie shell before chilling.

FRUIT IN LIQUEUR

1¾ cups (1-lb. can) drained peach slices
2 tablespoons creme de menthe
½ cup whipped topping

4 (½ cup) SERVINGS
124 Calories Each

In medium mixing bowl, combine peaches and creme de menthe; toss lightly to coat. Chill, covered, for 1 to 2 hours. Top each serving with 2 tablespoons whipped topping.

Tip: Any combinations of fruit and liqueur can be used.

Put this delightful dessert in the oven when you start eating dinner. It will be hot and ready to serve when you've finished your main course.

RUM RUMBA

1½ cups (1 large) sliced banana
1½ cups (2 med.) peeled and sectioned oranges*
2 tablespoons rum**

OVEN 300°

4 (⅔ cup) SERVINGS
102 Calories Each

Place banana slices in bottom of 8x8-inch baking pan or 1-quart casserole; top with orange sections. Drizzle rum over fruit. Bake at 300° for 20 to 25 minutes until hot and bubbly. Serve hot.

Tips: *Canned orange sections can be used for the fresh.

**If desired, 2 tablespoons water and ½ teaspoon rum flavoring can be used for the rum.

For those not watching calories, top serving with whipped topping or sweetened whipped cream.

Except for pineapple, frozen fruits may be substituted for fresh in any salad. Frozen pineapple can not be used in gelatin salads unless it is boiled, as it prevents the gelatin from thickening and becoming firm. If the frozen fruit is packed in syrup, drain the syrup before using the fruit in gelatin salads. Calorie counts for fruits canned in syrup or frozen with sugar will, of course, be higher.

CHILLED FRUIT CUP

1½ cups (13-oz. can) pineapple chunks
1 cup (1 med.) orange sections, cut in half
¾ cup fresh or frozen melon balls
⅔ cup (1 med.) banana slices
½ cup fresh halved strawberries
¼ cup lemon juice
2 tablespoons sugar

6 SERVINGS
96 Calories Each

Combine fruits. Blend lemon juice and sugar. Sprinkle over fruit and chill.

Tips: Any of the following combinations make a colorful and delicious fruit cup.

- Melon balls, pear halves and pineapple chunks with slices of fresh lime.
- Apricot halves, Royal Anne cherries and grapefruit sections.
- Purple plums and figs with thick, half slices of orange.
- Pineapple chunks, sliced peaches and fresh blueberries.
- Stewed prunes and apricot halves.
- Garnish fruit cup attractively with whole strawberries, mint leaves, maraschino cherries, frosted grapes, or lemon, orange or lime slices.

BAKED APPLES

6 baking apples, cored
6 tablespoons brown sugar
6 teaspoons butter or margarine
Cinnamon
1 cup water

OVEN 375°

6 SERVINGS
172 Calories Each

Remove peel around top of cored apples. Place in baking dish. Fill each center with 1 tablespoon brown sugar. Top each with 1 teaspoon butter. Sprinkle with cinnamon. Pour water around apples. Bake at 375° for 45 to 60 minutes until apples are tender.

Tip: For Sugar Glazed Apples: Melt 2 tablespoons butter or margarine. Roll apples in butter, then in mixture of ⅓ cup sugar and ½ teaspoon cinnamon. Sprinkle remaining mixture over apples. Bake as directed.

APPLESAUCE

4 cups (4 med.) peeled and sliced cooking apples
1¼ cups water
¼ cup sugar

4 (½ cup) SERVINGS
135 Calories Each

In large saucepan, combine apples and water. Cover; cook over low heat for 15 to 20 minutes, stirring occasionally, until tender. Stir in sugar. Serve warm or cold. Strain or sieve, if desired.

Tip: For Spicy Applesauce, add ½ teaspoon cinnamon and dash cloves with water.

BAKED BANANAS

6 firm bananas, peeled
1 tablespoon lemon juice
¼ cup firmly packed brown sugar
1 teaspoon cinnamon

OVEN 375°
6 SERVINGS
162 Calories Each

Place bananas in lightly greased baking dish. Sprinkle with lemon juice. Combine brown sugar and cinnamon, sprinkle over bananas. Bake at 375° for 18 to 20 minutes until bananas are tender.

Tip: For those not watching calories, serve with whipped cream or ice cream.

The Greeks considered ambrosia to be food for the gods. You'll know why when you taste this delightful combination.

AMBROSIA MEDLEY

2 cups (1 pt.) fresh strawberries, cut in half
2 cups fresh or canned pineapple tidbits
2 bananas, sliced
½ cup flaked coconut
¾ cup orange juice

8 (¾ cup) SERVINGS
95 Calories Each

Prepare fruits. Combine fruits; arrange with coconut in layers in large bowl. Sprinkle coconut on top. Drizzle with orange juice. Chill before serving.

Tip: For 4 servings, halve all ingredients.

Fruits baked with a delightful topping. Quick and easy, and you probably already have the ingredients on hand.

OVEN AMBROSIA

1 tablespoon butter or margarine
¼ cup grated coconut
2 tablespoons flour
2 tablespoons brown sugar
½ teaspoon salt
2 cups (1-lb. 4-oz. can) drained pineapple tidbits
2 cups (1-lb. 13-oz. can) drained sliced peaches

OVEN 400°
4 (⅔ cup) SERVINGS
281 Calories Each

While preheating oven, melt butter in 1½-quart casserole; remove from oven. Stir in coconut, flour, brown sugar and salt; mix thoroughly with fork. Add fruits; toss very lightly. Bake, uncovered, at 400° for 30 to 35 minutes until hot and bubbly. Serve warm. If desired, garnish with mint leaves.

Delicately flavored pears to give a refreshing end to a hearty or light meal.

PEARS IN WINE

2 cups (1-lb. can) drained pear halves
¼ cup red wine*
1 tablespoon grated lemon peel
½ teaspoon cinnamon

OVEN 350°
4 (½ cup) SERVINGS
90 Calories Each

In 8x8-inch baking dish or 1-quart casserole, combine all ingredients; mix well. Bake, uncovered, at 350° for 15 minutes until hot and bubbly. Serve hot or chill to serve cold.

Tips: *Orange or cranberry juice can be used for the red wine.

Fresh pears can be used for the canned pears.

For those not watching calories, top serving with sour cream, if desired.

To keep fresh fruits from turning dark, the friut may be brushed or dipped in lemon juice. Other citrus fruit juices, such as orange or lime, may also be used.

CREAMY PEACHES

2½ cups (I-lb. 13-oz. can) drained peach halves
Dash nutmeg
½ cup plain yogurt
2 tablespoons brown sugar

BROIL   6 SERVINGS
                            83 Calories Each

Place peach halves, cut-side down, in shallow dish or pie pan. Sprinkle with nutmeg. Cover with yogurt. Refrigerate several hours or overnight. Sprinkle with brown sugar. Place under broiler 2 to 5 minutes until sugar bubbles. Serve at once or chill until serving time.

CREAMY FRUIT MELANGE

1½ cups (2 med.) orange sections or pieces
I cup (I med.) banana slices
I cup (I med.) coarsely chopped apple
½ cup plain yogurt
I tablespoon sugar

                       6 (½ cup) SERVINGS
                            78 Calories Each

In medium mixing bowl, combine all ingredients; mix well. Chill until served.

Tip: Use ½ cup yogurt and I tablespoon sugar as a dressing for any of your favorite fruits.

A treat for the connoisseur, this dazzler is as fresh as spring with its mouth-watering strawberries and glossy glaze. A flourish of a finish for any meal.

STRAWBERRY GLACE

I tablespoon cornstarch
I teaspoon unsweetened lemon juice
⅓ cup sugar
⅔ cup water
5 drops red food coloring
2 drops yellow food coloring
4 cups (2 pts.) fresh strawberries, whole or halved

                          6 SERVINGS
                       85 Calories Each

In medium saucepan, combine all ingredients. Cook over medium heat, stirring constantly, until mixture thickens and starts to boil. Spoon warm glaze over berries. Spoon into serving dishes. Chill 1½ to 2 hours before serving.

Pears, cherries and apricots are baked with a combination of spices to give a refreshing dessert. Try with some fresh fruit, too.

SPICY FRUIT

2 cups (I-lb. can) drained pear halves
2 cups (I-lb. can) drained apricot halves
2 cups (I-lb. can) undrained pitted dark cherries
2 tablespoons sugar
½ teaspoon cinnamon
½ teaspoon ground ginger
⅛ to ¼ teaspoon ground cloves
2 tablespoons lemon juice

OVEN 350°   6 (½ cup) SERVINGS
                            183 Calories Each

In 2-quart casserole or baking dish, combine all ingredients; mix well. Bake, covered, at 350° for 25 to 30 minutes until hot and bubbly. Drain to serve hot or chill to serve cold.

Tip: Spicy Fruit can be made in a saucepan. Prepare as directed; heat over medium heat for 15 minutes until heated through.

Other combinations of fruits can be used; choose your favorites.

Spicy and sweet, this combination of fruits gives a zesty finish to your meal.

APRICOT-PLUM DESSERT

2 cups (I-lb. can) drained apricot halves, pits removed
2 cups (I-lb. can) drained purple plums, pits removed
2 tablespoons brown sugar
⅛ teaspoon nutmeg
¼ cup thinly sliced lemon wedges

                       6 (½ cup) SERVINGS
                            143 Calories Each

Combine all ingredients. Mix slightly. Heat and serve warm, or chill and serve cold. Remove lemon slices before serving.

Tip: Those watching calories may want a spoonfull of whipped topping or sour cream on top.

Peaches never had it so good! A hearty maple and cinnamon flavor makes a winner! Serve hot or cold for dessert or breakfast.

MAPLED PEACHES

   3½ **cups (1 lb. 13-oz. can) undrained peach slices**
   ½ **teaspoon maple flavoring**
   ¼ **teaspoon cinnamon**
   ⅛ **teaspoon ground nutmeg**

OVEN 350°   5 (½ cup) SERVINGS
                     71 Calories Each

In 8x8-inch baking dish or 1 to 1½-quart casserole, combine all ingredients; mix well. Bake, covered, at 350° for 15 minutes until hot and bubbly. Drain and serve. Or, chill and serve cold.

Tips: Mapled Peaches can be made in a saucepan. Prepare as directed; heat over medium heat 10 minutes until heated through.

For those not watching weight, top servings with sour cream or brown sugar, if desired.

A delicate chocolate dessert, velvety and fluffy — that will melt in your mouth. For those not watching calories, top with whipped topping. Or, set into a crust for a chocolate cream pie.

MOCK CHOCOLATE MOUSSE

   1 **tablespoon (1 envelope) unflavored gelatin**
   2 **cups skim milk**
   1 **tablespoon cornstarch**
   ¼ **cup sugar**
   1 **egg, separated**
   ⅓ **cup semi-sweet chocolate pieces**
   1 **teaspoon vanilla**
   ¼ **cup instant nonfat dry milk**
   ¼ **cup ice water***

          8 (½ cup) SERVINGS
            106 Calories Each

Chill small mixer bowl and beaters in refrigerator. In medium saucepan, soften gelatin in ½ cup of the skim milk. To the softened gelatin, add cornstarch, sugar, remaining 1½ cups skim milk, egg yolk and chocolate pieces. Cook over medium heat, stirring constantly, until mixture begins to thicken and comes to a boil. Remove from heat. Stir in vanilla. Chill until slightly thickened but not set. In small, chilled mixer bowl, beat nonfat dry milk, ice water and egg white at high speed until stiff peaks form. Fold into chocolate mixture. Carefully pour into serving dishes. Chill about 2 hours until firm.

Tip: *Place a few ice cubes in water until ice cold; this is essential for proper whipping.

SOFT CUSTARD

   2 **cups skim milk**
   3 **eggs, slightly beaten**
   ½ **cup sugar**
   ¼ **teaspoon salt**
   2 **teaspoons vanilla extract**

          6 (½ cup) SERVINGS
            133 Calories Each

In top of double boiler, combine milk, eggs, sugar and salt. Cook over rapidly boiling water, stirring constantly, until mixture coats a metal spoon. Remove from heat. Stir in vanilla extract. Chill rapidly. Pour into serving dishes, or serve as a sauce over sponge cake.

Tip: For Coconut Custard stir in ½ cup flaked coconut, plain or toasted, with vanilla extract.

Calorie Guide

MILK AND DAIRY PRODUCTS		Number of Calories

Cheese:

American, Cheddar-type ....1 oz.		115
	1-inch cube (3/5 oz.)....	70
	½ cup, grated (2 oz.)...	225
Process American, Cheddar-type.1 oz.		105
Blue-mold (or Roquefort-type) ..1 oz.		105
Cottage, not creamed..........2 tablespoons (1 oz.)....		25
Cottage, creamed ....2 tablespoons (1 oz.)....		30
Cottage, partially creamed.......2 tablespoons (1 oz.)....		25
Cream ....2 tablespoons (1 oz.)....		105
Neufchatel ....2 tablespoons (1 oz.)....		69
Parmesan, Dry, grated..........2 tablespoons (⅓ oz.)....		40
Swiss ....1 oz.		105

Cheese foods:

Cheddar ....1 oz.		90

Cream:

Light ....1 tablespoon		30
Heavy whipping ....1 tablespoon		55
Sour, dairy ....1 tablespoon		29
Yogurt (made from partially skimmed milk) ....1 cup		120

Dessert topping:

Aeresol ....1 tablespoon		10
Frozen ....1 tablespoon		16
Mix, prepared ....1 tablespoon		10

Ice cream:

Plain ....1 container (3½ oz.)		130
Ice milk ....½ cup (4 oz.).........		140
Ice cream soda, chocolate.......1 large glass		455

Milk:

Whole ....1 cup or glass.........		160
Skim (fresh or nonfat dry reconstituted) ....1 cup or glass.........		90
Buttermilk ....1 cup or glass.........		90
Evaporated (undiluted) ....½ cup		170
Condensed, sweetened (undiluted) ....½ cup		490
Half-and-Half (milk and cream)..1 cup		325
	1 tablespoon	20

Milk beverages:

Cocoa (all milk)................1 cup		235
Chocolate-flavored milk drink...1 cup		190
Malted milk ....1 cup		280
Chocolate milkshake ....One 12-oz. container....		520

MEATS, POULTRY AND EGGS		Number of Calories

Meat, cooked, without bone:

Beef:

Pot-roast or braised:

Lean and fat..................3 oz. (4x2½x½-in.).....245		
Lean only ....2½ oz. (4x2x½-in.).....140		

Oven roast:

Cut having relatively large proportion of fat to lean (rib or rump)

Lean and fat..................3 oz. (4x2½x½-in.).....375		
Lean only ....2 oz. (4x1½x½-in.).....140		

Cut having relatively low proportion of fat to lean (sirloin)

Lean and fat..................3 oz. (4x2½x½-in.).....165		
Lean only ....2½ oz. (4x2x½-in.).....115		

Rib roast:

Lean and fat..................3 oz. (4x2½x½-in.).....302		

Steak, broiled:

Lean and fat..................3 oz. (3x2½x1-in.).....260		
Lean only ....2 oz. (3x2½x1-in.).....128		

Steak, moist-cooked:
Round or family steak:

Lean and fat..................3 oz. (4x3x1-in.).......254		
Lean only ....2.7 oz. (4x3x1-in.).......173		

Brisket, lean and fat, braised or pot-roasted ....4 oz. (5x1x¼-in.).......411

Club steak, lean and fat, broiled...4 oz. 517

Flank Steak, pot-roasted..........4 oz. (5x1½x¾-in.).....223

Porterhouse steak, lean and fat, broiled ....8 oz. (½ lb.)..........242

Hamburger patty:
Regular ground round..........3-oz. patty (about 4 patties per lb. of raw meat)..........224

Lean ground round.............3-oz. patty (about 4 patties per lb. of raw meat)..........140

Corned beef, canned............3 oz. (3x2x1½-in.)......185

Lamb:

Chop (about 2½ chops per
lb., as purchased):
Lean and fat..................3½ oz. 318
Lean only ....2½ oz. 125
Roast, leg:
Lean and fat.................3 oz. (3½x3x½-in.).....235
Lean only ....2½ oz. (3½x2½x½-in.). 130
Shoulder, lean and fat, roasted...4 oz. (4x3x½-in.).......385

Pork:

Fresh:
Chop (about 3 chops per lb.
as purchased):
Lean and fat.................2½ oz. 286
Lean only ....2 oz. 155
Roast, loin:
Lean and fat.................3 oz. (4x2½x½-in.).....310
Lean only ....2 2/5 oz. (3x2½x½-in.).. 175
Boston butt, lean and fat,
roasted ....3 oz. (3x2xl-in.).......328
Spareribs, braised ....4 oz. 499
Cured (Ham):
Lean and fat.................3 oz. (4x2x½-in.)......254
Lean only ....2 1/5 oz. (4x3½x½-in) .. 167
Bacon, broiled or fried........1 thin slice 48

Sausage, Variety and Luncheon Meats:

Bologna sausage ....1 oz. (4½x⅛-in.) 87
Liver sausage (liverwurst).......2 oz. (3-in. diameter
x½-in.) 158
Vienna sausage, canned........2 oz. (4 to 5 sausages)... 127
Pork sausage, link............1 link (½-in. diameter
x3-in.) 94
Wiener ....1 wiener 155
Boiled ham (luncheon meat).....2 oz. (3½x3x¼-in.) 135
Spiced ham, canned...........2 oz. (3x2½x¼-in.) ... 165

Poultry, cooked, without bone:
Chicken:

Broiled ....3 oz. (about ¼ of a
small broiler) 185
Fried ....½ breast, 3 oz. 232
thigh and drumstick,
3 oz. 225
Canned ....3½ oz. (½ cup)........ 178
Roasted:
Light meat ....3½ oz. (3x2¼x¾-in.)... 198
Dark meat ....4 oz. (3x2¼x¾-in.) 210
Poultry pie (with potatoes, peas
and gravy) ....1 small pie
(4¼ in. diameter)....535

Turkey:

Roasted:
Light meat ....4 oz. (3x2½x¾-in.).....200
Dark meat ....4 oz. (3x2½x¾-in.).....230

Fish and shellfish:

Bluefish, baked ....3 oz. (3½x2x½-in.) 135
Clams, shelled:
Raw, meat only...............3 oz.
(about 4 med. clams).. 65
Canned, clams and juice.......3 oz., ½ cup.......... 52
Crab meat, canned or cooked...3 oz., ½ cup.......... 85
Fish sticks, breaded, cooked,
frozen (including breading and
fat for frying)..............4 oz. (5 fish sticks).....200
Flounder, fillet, broiled........4 oz. (4x2xl-in.) 170
Haddock, fried (including fat for
frying) ....4 oz. (3x3x½-in.) 165
Broiled ....4 oz. (4x3x½-in.) 100
Halibut, fresh broiled..........4 oz. (4x3x¾-in.) 214
Lobster, boiled or broiled.......¾ lb. plus 2 tbsp. butter 308
Canned ....½ cup 85

Mackerel:

Broiled ....3 oz. (4x3x½ in.).......200
Canned ....3 oz. solids and liquid
(about 3/5 cup)...... 155
Ocean perch, fried (including
egg, breadcrumbs, and fat
for frying) ....3 oz. (4x2½x½-in.)..... 195
Oysters, shucked:
Raw meat only...............½ cup (6 to 10 med.
oysters, selects) 80

Salmon:

Broiled or baked............4 oz. (4½x2½x½-in.)...205
Canned (pink) ....3 oz. solids and liquid,
(about 3/5 cup)...... 120
Sardines, canned in oil..........3 oz. drained solids
(5 to 7 med. sardines). 175
Shrimp, canned, meat only......3 oz. (about 17 med.
shrimp) 100
Swordfish ....4 oz. (3x3x¾-in.)...... 127
Tunafish, canned in oil, meat
only ....3 oz. (about ½ cup)....170
canned in water............3 oz. (about ½ cup)....127

Eggs:

Fried (including fat for frying)...1 large egg............ 100
Hard or soft cooked, boiled ....1 large egg............ 80
Scrambled or omelet (including
milk and fat for cooking).......1 large egg............ 110
Poached ....1 large egg............ 80

Dry beans and peas:

Red kidney beans,
canned or cooked............½ cup, solids and liquid 115
Lima, cooked ....½ cup, solids and liquid 130
Baked beans, with tomato or
molasses:
With pork ....½ cup 160
Without pork ....½ cup 155

Nuts:

Almonds, shelled ....2 tablespoons (about 13 to
15 almonds) 105
Brazil nuts, shelled, broken
pieces ....2 tablespoons 115
Cashew nuts, roasted..........2 tablespoons (about 4 to
5 nuts) 95
Coconut:
Fresh, shredded meat.........2 tablespoons 40
Dried, shredded, sweetened....2 tablespoons 45
Peanuts, roasted, shelled........2 tablespoons 105
Peanut butter ....1 tablespoon 95
Pecans, shelled halves..........2 tablespoons (about
12 to 14 halves)....... 95
Walnuts, shelled:
Black or native, chopped.......2 tablespoons 100
English or Persian, halves......2 tablespoons (about
7 to 12 halves)....... 80

Corned beef hash, canned......3 oz. (scant half cup)... 155
Dried beef, chipped............2 oz. (about ⅓ cup).... 115
Meat loaf ....2 oz. (4x2½x½-in.).... 115
Beef and vegetable stew........½ cup 105
Beef potpie, baked............1 pie (4¼-in. diameter)..560
Chili con carne, canned:
Without beans ....½ cup 255
With beans ....½ cup 170

Veal:

Cutlet, broiled meat only........3 oz. (4x2½x½-in.).....185
Chop, broiled ....4 oz. 267
Rib, roasted ....4 oz. (4x3x½-in.).......305
Round with rump, broiled......4 oz. (4x2½x½-in.)....245

Artichokes:
Fresh, cooked ....1 med. 30
Hearts, frozen ....2 hearts 22

Asparagus:
Cooked or canned............6 med. spears or ½ cup
cut spears 20
Frozen ....½ cup 25

Bamboo shoots, canned ....½ cup 30

Bean sprouts ....½ cup 10

Beans:
Lima, green, cooked or canned..½ cup 80
Frozen ....½ cup 96
Snap, green, wax or yellow,
cooked or canned............½ cup 15
Baked ....½ cup 180
Butterbeans, frozen ....½ cup 313
Red kidney ....½ cup 115

Beets, cooked or canned........½ cup, chopped....... 30

Beet greens, cooked.........½ cup 15

Broccoli:
Cooked ....½ cup flower stalks..... 20
Frozen ....½ cup 27

Brussels sprouts:
Cooked ....½ cup 20
Frozen ....½ cup 24

Cabbage:
Raw ....½ cup, shredded....... 10
1 wedge (3½x4½-in.)... 25
Cooked ....½ cup 20
Coleslaw (with mayonnaise-
type salad dressing)...........½ cup 60
Chinese, raw ....½ cup 7
Sauerkraut ....½ cup 23

Carrots:
Raw ....1 carrot (5½x1-in.
diameter) 20
½ cup, grated......... 20
Cooked ....½ cup, chopped 20

Cauliflower:
Cooked ....½ cup flower buds..... 10
Raw ....½ cup 13
Frozen ....½ cup 21

Celery, raw ....2 large stalks (8-in. long)
or 3 small stalks
(5-in. long) 10

Chard, cooked ....½ cup 15

Collards, cooked ....½ cup 30

Corn:
On cob, cooked...............1 ear (5-in. long) 70
Kernels, cooked or canned......½ cup 85
Cut, frozen ....½ cup 75

Cress, garden, cooked..........½ cup 20

Cucumber, peeled ....6 slices (⅛-in thick) 5

Eggplant, cooked ....2 slices, ½ cup chopped 19

Kale, cooked ....½ cup 15

Kohlrabi, cooked ....½ cup 20

Lettuce, raw ....2 large or 4 small leaves 10

Mushrooms:
Fresh ....½ cup 14
Canned ....½ cup 20

Mustard greens, cooked.........½ cup 20

Okra:
Cooked ....4 pods 10
Frozen ....½ cup 36

Onions:
Young, green, raw.............6 small, without tops.... 20
Mature: raw ....1 onion (2½-in. diameter) 40
1 tablespoon, chopped.. 5
Cooked ....½ cup 30

Parsley, raw, chopped..........1 tablespoon 1

Parsnips, cooked ....½ cup 50

Peas:
Green, canned ....½ cup 60
Frozen ....½ cup 70
Fresh ....½ cup 57
Black-eye, frozen, cooked.......½ cup 95
And carrots, frozen............½ cup 52

Peppers, green:
Raw or cooked..............1 med. 10

Pimiento, canned ....1 med. 10

Potatoes:
Baked ....1 med. (2½-in. diameter) 90
Boiled ....½ cup, chopped....... 50
Chips (including fat for frying)...10 med. (2-in. diameter). 115
French-fried (including fat for
frying)
Ready-to-eat ....10 pieces (2x½x½-in.)... 155
Frozen, heated, ready-to-serve...10 pieces (2x½x½-in.)... 125

Potatoes: (continued)

Hash-browned ....½ cup 225
Mashed:
  Milk added ....½ cup 60
  Milk and fat added ....½ cup 90
Pan-fried, beginning with raw
  potatoes ....½ cup 230

Radishes, raw ....4 small 5

Sauerkraut, canned ....½ cup 20

Spinach:

Cooked or canned ....½ cup 20
Frozen ....½ cup 23

Squash:

Summer:
  Fresh, cooked ....½ cup 15
  Frozen ....½ cup 20
Winter:
  Baked, mashed ....½ cup 65
  Frozen ....½ cup 45

Sweet potatoes:

Baked in jacket ....1 med. (5x2-in.)........ 155
Canned, vacuum or solid pack...½ cup 120

Tomatoes:

Raw ....1 med. (2x2½-in.)....... 35
Cooked or canned ....½ cup 25
Juice, canned ....½ cup 20
Sauce ....½ cup 52
Paste ....½ cup 123
Puree ....½ cup 59

Turnips, cooked ....½ cup 20

Turnip greens, cooked ....½ cup 15

Apples:

Fresh ....1 med. (2½-in. diameter) 70
Applejuice, canned ....½ cup 60
Applesauce:
  Sweetened ....½ cup 115
  Unsweetened ....½ cup 50

Apricots:

Fresh ....3 (about 12 per lb., as
      purchased) 55
Canned:
  Water pack ....½ cup, halves and liquid 45
  Heavy syrup pack.............½ cup, halves and syrup 110
Dried, cooked, unsweetened....½ cup, fruit and juice.. 120
Frozen, sweetened ....½ cup 125

Avocados:

California varieties ....½ of a 10-oz. avocado
      (3⅓x4¼-in.) 185
Florida varieties ....½ of a 13-oz. avocado
      (4x3-in.) 160

Bananas, fresh ....1 banana (6x1½-in.)..... 85

Berries:

Blackberries, fresh ....½ cup 40
Blueberries, fresh ....½ cup 40
Raspberries:
  Fresh, red ....½ cup 35
  Frozen, red, sweetened........½ cup 120
  Fresh, black ....½ cup 50
Strawberries:
  Fresh ....½ cup 30
  Frozen, sweetened ....½ cup, sliced....... 140

Cantaloupe, fresh ....½ melon (5-in. diameter) 60

Cherries:

Fresh:
  Sour ....½ cup 30
  Sweet ....½ cup 40
  Frozen Bing ....½ cup 124
  Maraschino ....1 cherry 20

Cranberry:

Sauce, canned, sweetened.......1 tablespoon 25
Juice cocktail ....½ cup 80

Dates, "fresh" and dried,
pitted, cut . . . . ½ cup 245

Figs:
Fresh . . . . 3 small (1½-in. diameter,
about ¼ lb.) 90
Canned, heavy syrup . . . . ½ cup 110
Dried . . . . 1 large (2x1-in.) 60

Fruit cocktail:
Canned in heavy syrup . . . . ½ cup 100
Fresh, dairy packed . . . . ½ cup 68

Grapefruit:
Fresh:
White . . . . ½ med. (4¼-in.
diameter) 55
½ cup sections 40
Pink or red . . . . ½ med. (4¼-in.
diameter) 60
Canned:
Water pack . . . . ½ cup 35
Syrup pack . . . . ½ cup 90
Frozen concentrate, diluted,
ready-to-serve:
Unsweetened . . . . ½ cup 50
Sweetened . . . . ½ cup 60

Grapes, fresh:
Concord, Delaware, Niagara and
Scuppernong . . . . 1 cup, with skins and
seeds 65
Malaga, Muscat, Thompson
Seedless and Flame Tokay . . . . . 1 cup, with skins and
seeds 95
Grapejuice, bottled . . . . ½ cup 80

Honeydew melon:
Fresh . . . . 1 wedge (2x7-in.) 50
Melon balls, frozen . . . . ¾ cup 72

Lemons:
Juice, raw or canned . . . . ½ cup 30
1 tablespoon 5
Lemonade, frozen concentrate,
sweetened, diluted, ready-to-
serve . . . . ½ cup 55

Lime juice, fresh . . . . 1 tablespoon 8

Oranges:
Fresh . . . . 1 orange (3-in. diameter). 75
Mandarin, canned . . . . ⅓ cup 55

Orange Juice:
Fresh . . . . ½ cup 55
Canned, unsweetened . . . . ½ cup 60
Frozen concentrate, diluted,
ready-to-serve . . . . ½ cup 55
Orange-Grapefruit, frozen . . . . . . ¾ cup 84

Peaches:
Fresh . . . . 1 med. (2-in. diameter) . . 35
½ cup, sliced 30
Canned:
Water pack . . . . ½ cup 40
Heavy syrup pack . . . . ½ cup 100
Dried, cooked, unsweetened . . . . ½ cup (5 to 6 halves and
3 tablespoons syrup) . . 110
Frozen, sweetened . . . . ½ cup 105

Pears:
Fresh . . . . 1 pear (3x2½-in.
diameter) 100
Canned in heavy syrup . . . . ½ cup 100

Pineapple:
Fresh . . . . ½ cup, chunks 40
Chunks, canned in own juice . . . . ½ cup 64
Canned in heavy syrup:
Crushed . . . . ½ cup 100
Sliced . . . . 2 small or 1 large slice
and 2 tablespoons
juice 90
Pineapple juice, canned . . . . ½ cup 70

Papaya, fresh . . . . ½ cup 35

Plums:
Fresh . . . . 1 plum (2-in. diameter) . . 25
Canned, syrup pack . . . . ½ cup 100

Prunes, dried, cooked:
Unsweetened . . . . ½ cup (8 to 9 prunes and
2 tablespoons liquid) . . 150
Sweetened . . . . ½ cup (8 to 9 prunes and
2 tablespoons liquid) . . 255
Stewed . . . . ½ cup 100
Prune juice, canned . . . . ½ cup 100

Raisins, dried . . . . ½ cup 230

Rhubarb:
Cooked, sweetened . . . . ½ cup 190
Frozen . . . . ½ cup 84

Tangerine:
Fresh . . . . 1 med. (2½-in. diameter) 40
Tangerine juice:
Canned . . . . ½ cup 50
Frozen . . . . ¾ cup 85

Watermelon, fresh . . . . 1 wedge (4x8-in. long) . . 115

Number of Calories

Barley, pearl, uncooked..........¼ cup 177

Bread:

Cracked wheat ....1 slice, ½-in. thick...... 60
French, enriched ....1 slice, ½-in. thick...... 60
Pumpernickle ....1 slice, ½-in. thick...... 79
Raisin ....1 slice, ½-in. thick...... 60
Rye ....1 slice, ½-in. thick...... 55
White ....1 slice, ½-in. thick...... 60
Whole wheat ....1 slice, ½-in. thick...... 55

Breadcrumbs ....¼ cup 86

Cereals:

Bran flakes (40% bran)..........1 oz. (about 4/5 cup).... 85
Corn, puffed, presweetened.....1 oz. (1 cup)........... 110
 Corngrits, cooked ....¾ cup 90
 Flakes ....1 oz. (about 1⅓ cups)... 110
Farina, cooked ....¾ cup 75
Grapenut flakes ....1 oz. 110
Oats, puffed or flakes..........1 oz. (about 1 cup)..... 115
Oatmeal, cooked ....¾ cup 100
Rice flakes ....1 oz. (1 cup)........... 115
 Puffed ....½ oz. (1 cup)......... 55
Wheat, rolled, cooked..........¾ cup 130
 Shredded ....1 oz. (1 large biscuit or
                            about ½ cup bite-
                            sized) 100
 Puffed ....1 oz. (about 2⅛ cups)... 105
 Puffed, presweetened ....1 oz. (about 2 cups)..... 105
 Flakes ....1 oz. (about ¾ cup) 100
 Germ ....¾ cup 185

Corn Chips ....1 oz. 166

Cornmeal, white or yellow:
Unenriched ....1 cup 420
Enriched ....1 cup 525

Macaroni, cooked:
Enriched ....½ cup 80
Unenriched ....½ cup 80
Macaroni and cheese..........½ cup 235

Noodles, cooked:
Enriched ....½ cup 100
Unenriched ....½ cup 100

Other baked goods:
Baking powder biscuit..........1 biscuit (2½-in.
                             diameter) 140
Crackers:
 Graham ....4 small or 2 med. 55
 Rye wafers ....2 wafers (1⅞x3½-in.)... 45
 Saltines ....2 crackers (2 in. square). 35
 Soda ....2 crackers (2½ in.
                             square) 50
 Oyster ....10 crackers 45
Doughnuts (cake type)..........1 doughnut 125
Muffins:
 Plain ....1 muffin (2¾-in.
                             diameter) 140
 Bran ....1 muffin (2¾-in.
                             diameter) 130
 Corn ....1 muffin (2¾-in.
                             diameter) 150
 English ....1 muffin 145

Number of Calories

Pizza (cheese) ....5½-in. sector (⅛ of a
                            14-in. pie) 185

Pretzels ....5 small sticks......... 20

Rice, cooked:
Brown ....⅔ cup 100
White ....½ cup 92
Wild ....½ cup 73

Rolls:
Plain, pan ....1 roll (16 oz. per dozen). 115
Hard, round ....1 roll (22 oz. per dozen). 160
Sweet, pan ....1 roll (18 oz. per dozen). 135
Spaghetti, cooked ....½ cup 77
 In tomato sauce............1 cup with cheese.......260
 In tomato-meat sauce..........1 cup 396

Waffles ....1 waffle (4½x5½x½-in.) 210

Wheat flours:
All purpose ....1 cup 400
Cake or pastry flour............1 cup 365
Self-rising ....1 cup 385
Whole wheat ....1 cup 400

Yeast, brewer's dry.............1 tablespoon 25

Brownies 1 (1½x1½x¾-in.) 120

Cakes:

Angelfood cake .... 2-in. sector (1/12 of 8-in.
round cake) 110

Butter cakes:

Plain, without icing........... 1 piece (3x2x1½-in.) 200
1 cupcake, 2¾-in.
diameter 145

Plain, with chocolate icing..... 2-in. sector (1/16 of 10-in.
round layer cake) 370
1 cupcake, 2¾-in.
diameter 185

Chocolate, with chocolate
icing .... 2-in. sector (1/16 of 10-in.
round layer cake).....445

Fruitcake, dark .... 1 piece (2x2x½-in.) 115

Gingerbread .... 1 piece (2x2-in.) 175

Pound cake .... 1 slice (2¾x3x⅝-in.)... 140

Sponge cake .... 2-in. sector (1/12 of 8-in.
round cake) 120

Cookies:

Plain and assorted .... 1 cookie (3-in. diameter). 120

Chocolate wafer .... 1 (2⅜-in. diameter) 36

Creme sandwich, chocolate..... 1 54

Figbars, small .... 1 figbar 55

Gingersnaps .... 1 (3-in. diameter) 52

Sugar wafer 1 (2x¾x¼-in.) 10

Vanilla wafer 1 22

Custard, baked .... ½ cup 140

Gelatin, unflavored .... 1 tablespoon (1 envelope) 35

Gelatin dessert, plain, ready-
to-serve .... ½ cup 70

Ice cream:

Plain .... 1 container (3½ oz.) 130

Ice milk .... ½ cup (4 oz.) 140

Fruit ice .... ½ cup 75

Pies:

Apple .... 4-in. sector (1/7 of 9-in.
pie) 345

Lemon Meringue .... 4-in. sector (1/7 of 9-in.
pie) 305

Pumpkin .... 4-in. sector (1/7 of 9-in.
pie) 275

Frozen:

Fruit varieties .... ⅛ pie ....151 to 193

Cream varieties .... ⅛ pie ....157 to 195

Pie crust:

Plain, baked .... 1 9-in. crust...........675

Puddings:

Chocolate .... ½ cup 219

Cornstarch pudding .... ½ cup 140

Lemon snow .... ¾ cup 114

Tapioca .... ½ cup 181

Vanilla .... ½ cup 187

Rennet dessert pudding,
ready-to-serve .... ½ cup 130

Sherbet .... ½ cup 130

Strudels, frozen .... 1 slice (1/6) 213

Turnovers, frozen .... 3 oz. 290

SOUPS

Number of
Calories

Bean with pork .... 1 cup 170

Beef noodle .... 1 cup 70

Bouillon, broth, and consomme.. 1 cup 30

Chicken noodle .... 1 cup 65

Clam chowder .... 1 cup 85

Cream of asparagus .... 1 cup 155

Cream of mushroom .... 1 cup 135

Minestrone .... 1 cup 105

Onion soup mix, dry .... 1 envelope or can 150

Oyster stew .... 1 cup (3 to 4 oysters)....200

Pea, green .... 1 cup 130

Tomato .... 1 cup 90

Vegetable with beef broth ...... 1 cup 80

SUGARS, SWEETS, AND RELATED PRODUCTS

Number of
Calories

Candy:

Butterscotch .... 1 piece 21

Caramels .... 1 oz. (3 med. caramels).. 115

Chocolate creams .... 1 oz. (2 to 3 pieces,
35 per lb.) 125

Chocolate, milk, sweetened ..... 1 oz. bar 150

Chocolate, milk, sweetened
with almonds .... 1 oz. bar 150

Chocolate mints .... 1 oz. (1 to 2 mints,
20 per lb.) 115

Fudge, milk chocolate, plain .... 1 oz. (1 piece, 1 to 1½
in. square) 115

Gumdrops .... 1 oz. (about 2½ large
or 20 small) 100

Hard candy .... 1 oz. (3 to 4 candy balls
¾-in. diameter) 110

Jellybeans .... 1 oz. (10 beans) 105

Marshmallows .... 1 oz. (3 to 4 marshmallows 60 per lb.) ... 90

Peanut brittle .... 1 oz. (1½ pieces, 2½ x
1¼x⅜-in. 120

Sirup, honey, molasses:

Chocolate sirup .... 1 tablespoon 50

Honey, strained or extracted ....1 tablespoon 65

Molasses:

Cane, light sirup .... 1 tablespoon 50

Black strap .... 1 tablespoon 45

Sirup, table blends .... 1 tablespoon 60

Jelly .... 1 tablespoon 55

Jam, marmalade, preserves .... 1 tablespoon 55

Sugar: White, granulated,
or brown .... 1 tablespoon 15

Powdered .... 1 tablespoon 31

BEVERAGES

Number of Calories

Alcoholic beverages:

Beer, 3.6% alcohol by weight....8-oz. glass 100
Brandy ....1½ oz. 75
Liqueurs ....1 oz. 165
Manhattan ....2½ oz. 165
Martini ....2½ oz. 145
Whisky, gin, rum:
  100-proof ....1 jigger (1½ oz.) 125
  90-proof ....1 jigger (1½ oz.) 110
  86-proof ....1 jigger (1½ oz.) 105
  80-proof ....1 jigger (1½ oz.) 100
  70-proof ....1 jigger (1½ oz.) 85
Wines:
  Table wines (such as Chablis,
  Claret, Rhine wine, and
  Sauterne) ....1 wine glass (about 3 oz.) 75
  Dessert wines (such as Muscatel,
  Port, Sherry, and Tokay)........1 wine glass (about 3 oz.) 125

Carbonated beverages:

Ginger Ale ....8-oz. glass 70
Cola-type ....8-oz. glass 95

Fruit juices, see Fruits

FATS, OILS & RELATED PRODUCTS

Number of Calories

Butter or margarine ....1 tablespoon 100
  1 pat or square 50
  (64 per lb.)

Cooking fats:

Vegetable ....1 tablespoon 110
Lard ....1 tablespoon 125

Salad or cooking oils ....1 tablespoon 125

Salad dressings:

French ....1 tablespoon 60
Blue cheese, French ....1 tablespoon 80
Home-cooked, boiled ....1 tablespoon 30
Low-calorie ....1 tablespoon 15
Mayonnaise ....1 tablespoon 110
Salad dressing, commercial,
  plain (mayonnaise-type) ....1 tablespoon 65
Thousand Island ....1 tablespoon 75
Vinegar ....1 tablespoon 2

Relishes:

Tomato catsup ....1 tablespoon 15
Mustard ....1 tablespoon 10

Sauces:

Barbecue sauce ....1 tablespoon 17
Chili sauce ....1 tablespoon 17
Spaghetti, canned ....½ cup 72
Mix, prepared ....½ cup 83
Tartar ....1 tablespoon 72
Worcestershire sauce ....1 tablespoon 14

MISCELLANEOUS

Number of Calories

Bouillon cube ....1 cube or 1 teaspoon.... 6

Cocoa powder ....1 tablespoon 21

Coconut:

Dried, shredded ....½ cup 170
Fresh ....½ cup 167

Olives:

Green ....4 med. or 3 extra large
  or 2 giant 15
Ripe ....3 small or 2 large 15

Pickles, cucumber:

Dill ....1 large, (4-in.x1¾-in.
  diameter) 15
Sweet ....1 pickle, (2¾-in.x¾-in.
  diameter) 30

Popcorn, popped (with oil and
salt added) ....1 cup 65

Sauces:

Gravy ....2 tablespoons 35
White sauce, medium (1 cup
  milk, 2 tbsp. fat, and
  2 tbsp. flour) ....½ cup 215
Cheese sauce (medium white
  sauce with 2 tbsp. cheese
  per cup ....½ cup 245

T.V. Dinners:

Chicken, fried ....11 oz. 435
Beef ....11 oz. 350
Turkey ....11 oz. 334
Macaroni and cheese ....12.4 oz. 375

Index